101 Dance Games
for Children

Other Smart Fun Books:

101 Music Games by Jerry Storms

101 Drama Games by Paul Rooyackers (forthcoming)

101 Movement Games by Huberta Wiertsema (forthcoming)

101
Dance Games FOR Children

Fun and Creativity with Movement

Paul Rooyackers

Illustrated by Cecilia Hurd

a **Hunter House** *Smart Fun* **book**

First published in The Netherlands in 1992 by Panta Rhei as
Honderd Dansspelen

Library of Congress Cataloging-in-Publication Data
Rooyackers, Paul
101 dance games for children : fun and creativity with movement /
Paul Rooyackers.
p. cm.
Includes index.
ISBN 0-89793-171-8 (pbk.). — ISBN 0-89793-172-6 (spiral)
1. Games. 2. Dancing for children. I. Title.
GV1203.R59 1995
790.1'922—dc20 95-13201
CIP

Project Manager: Lisa Lee   Production Manager: Paul J. Frindt
Cover design: Jil Weil Graphic Design   Book Design: Dian-Aziza Ooka
Illustrations: Cecilia Hurd   Translated by: Panta Rhei Katwijk
Editors: Colleen Paretty, Rosemary Wallner   Proofreader: Susan Burckhard
Sales & Marketing: Corrine M. Sahli   Publicity & Promotion: Darcy Cohan
Customer Support: Joshua Tabisaura
Order Fulfillment: A & A Quality Shipping Services
Administration: María Jesús Aguiló
Publisher: Kiran S. Rana

Typeset in Charter by 847 Communications, Alameda CA
Printed and bound by Data Reproductions, Rochester Hills MI
Manufactured in the United States of America
9 8 7 6 5 4 3 2 1   First edition

Contents

A detailed list of games with appropriate age levels
starts on the next page.

List of Games

	Young children	Older children	Teens to adults

List of Games, continued

List of Games, continued

List of Games, continued

Preface

Anyone can dance—young children, older children, teens, and adults. The universal, cross-cultural language of dance can also broaden the personal, creative, physical, and social education of the players, no matter where they live or who they are.

This book is written for anyone interested in leading a group of children in one or more dance games: teachers, parents, childcare workers, playground supervisors, babysitters, older relatives and siblings—anyone who wishes to pass along the infectious joy of dancing. These dance games can be used in the classroom, on the playground, during a gymnastics class, or in a music lesson. In simple settings and family situations, they offer loads of possibilities as independent, fun-filled activities.

This book is organized in two parts. "Beginnings," is a short discussion about dance, play, and dance games. It elucidates what dance is, the value of dance for a group, how to approach a particular dance, and the aim of dance games. It explains the leader's role, especially how to choose a dance game and prepare for it, and the significance of the structure and organization of the activity itself.

The second part, "Let's Dance," is a collection of dance games divided into eleven sections, each based on a particular theme or characteristic. All are designed to bring as much variety and amusement as possible to your dance activities.

These dance games have been gathered or created over a number of years. I would never have been able to develop them without the participation and enthusiasm of the many players, young and old. This book is dedicated to all the children and adults with whom I have been able to work—and dance.

Paul Rooyackers
The Netherlands, 1996

Beginnings

The Benefits of Playing and Dancing

Play is important. It gives us a chance to put daily concerns aside and become completely engrossed in another world. When you play, you travel outside reality for a time and behave as if your world is different. You could assume a different identity and slip inside someone else's skin. You could imagine living in another place or in a different setting. Each type of play teaches a new experience, a new vision, and opens a window into another reality. When you play you can make mistakes, make dreams come true, and laugh at yourself—all without anyone blaming you. People sometimes assume playing is just for young children, but play is possible—and vital—for everyone.

Dancing is a particularly enjoyable way to play, and you don't need years of experience to dance. The technique of a Rudolf Nureyev or a Fred Astaire is not necessary for most of us to realize the sheer joy of moving our bodies. For dancing is life: Anyone who doesn't know the joy of dancing is only half alive. Dance was probably one of the first forms of communication and modern times have not changed the indisputable fact that you can talk with your body; it has its own language and can relay information to others via posture and movement. Here are a few of the benefits of dance:

- Dance is relaxing. When your body feels good, it expresses itself with ease. People who feel comfortable with their body tend to get along well with others and interact with them in a relaxed manner.

- Dance encourages creativity. When you dance, you explore the world around you. You discover how you can use your body to be creative and communicate with others. You learn to put out your "feelers" and know when another person is kind, hostile, or eager to move along with you. When you dance, you improvise, translating your thoughts and feelings into movements.

- Dance develops your personality. Dancing allows you to improve your ability to perform; you gain more control over what you do and what you intend to do. You develop more self-confidence.

- Dance improves your social and emotional growth. Self-knowledge is a by-product of dance, and you dare to express more with your body and take more risks when you have a better sense of who you are. Because dance asks you to concentrate on your body while it is in unfamiliar positions, it encourages you to break through common roles and patterns.

- Dance trains your body. Your body is never completely still; some part of it is always moving. You must learn to take care of your body beyond the basic tasks of feeding, washing, and resting it. You must also learn to know the limits of your stamina and how to move correctly to avoid injury. Dance develops muscle strength and increases energy levels; it teaches you about your body in relation to space; it teaches you how to control movement and speed.

The games in this book combine play and dance, enhancing the pleasant escapism of play with the expressive qualities of dance. Although written with children in mind, anyone can benefit from these games.

Who Should Use This Book

This book is for parents who have a group of children in their house or yard who need entertaining, whether it's party time, vacation time, or family time; physical education and other teachers, preschool and kindergarten through high school; camp counselors involved with any age group; cub scout and girl scout leaders; day care centers; church groups, and everyone else who leads children in play and is looking for new ways to amuse and educate them.

None of these games calls for dividing the group into those who are unskilled and those who are dancers. Nor do they require that the children know how to dance.

You, the group leader, will not need any dance experience or expertise either. All you need is enthusiasm, commitment, adaptability, and the ability to work with groups of children of all sizes and ages, and the openness to share their enjoyment of the movements and dances they make.

The Role of the Leader

Prepare the class

As the leader, you choose the dances, consult colleagues and participants if appropriate, and stimulate the group while the dance game proceeds. You gather props, introduce the game, explain any rules and objectives, provide guidance where necessary, and end the game. When leading a game, watch the players and listen to them; find out the group's level of skill.

Know the participants

You need to know what kind of group you are working with. How large is the group? What are their ages? What is the ideal size for the dance game you're planning? Is the number of participants suitable for the amount of space you have to work in? Is the group already familiar with dance? If so, where have they gained this experience? How long have they been working together? What kinds of themes has the group worked with? How is the group made up? Is it all girls, all boys, or mixed?

Ask in advance if there are any participants who can't take part in the games because of a particular disability or on a doctor's advice, for example. The participants don't have to answer your question in front of the whole group; ask in advance so that individual participants can let you know. With dance, as with sports, prevention is better than cure.

Be flexible

You may need to adjust parts of the game based on how many players you have and on time and other constraints. Players may want to begin a game from a different part of the room. Develop an overview of the entire program and familiarize yourself with each dance game.

The importance of tone of voice

Introduce each dance game with care. Your tone of voice and choice of words will determine whether instructions come across clearly or muddled. You will also show your enthusiasm about the dance and its performance. Work with the warmth and volume of your voice to achieve the best clarity and most encouragement possible.

Choosing a Dance Game

Make sure the game is appropriate

If you know when, where, and with whom you'll be dancing or leading, read through this book and begin to think about suitable dance games. Refer to the "List of Games" on pages vi–x for appropriate age levels, and keep in mind that games can be adapted easily. Think about what you want the participants to do and experience. Make sure the proper space is available. Be prepared to adapt the dance game to the abilities of the participants.

There are dance games here for all kinds of gatherings. The introduction games in the first section are particularly suitable for a group whose members don't know each other well. The story and party dances can be extended or adapted at will. When choosing a dance game, consider the amount of time you have and the combination of dance games selected.

How the dance games are organized

The games in this book are organized into eleven sections, but feel free to combine the games from one section with those from another section. Combine a hand dance with a cooperation or concentration dance, for example. Interchange themes. A hand dance may have a theme about possessions and greed, but you can add another image from experiences in your own life, such as meeting someone who will not let you go.

Within a section, the games progress and develop from the first to the last. Most of the dance games also include variations, and very often these are simply additional ways of developing the game's theme.

Icons used with the games

To help you find games suitable for a particular time period and group, all the games are coded with symbols or icons. These icons tell you at a glance some things about the game:

the appropriate age group

the amount of time needed

the size of the group needed

the props required

the space required

These are explained in more detail below and a full listing of the icons is given on page 11.

Suitability in terms of age   These indicate the difference between games for young children, older children, and teenagers.

Young children (up to age 8)

Older children (ages 9 through 12)

Teenagers (12 and up)

All ages

How long the game takes   The games are divided into those that require about 5 minutes, those that take 10 to 20 minutes, those that take 30 minutes or more.

About 5 minutes

 10 to 20 minutes

 30 minutes or more

The size of the group needed   While some games require an even number of players or multiples of threes or fours, you can play many of the games with any sized group.

 Even number

 Multiples of 3 (can be divided into groups of 3)

 Multiples of 4

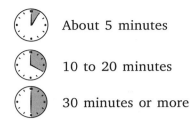 Group size open

Whether you need props   Some games require the use of props, such as boxes, streamers, ribbons, or feathers. Others require some kind of teaching aid, such as photographs of animals or storybooks.

Props needed

Large space needed   While a large space is ideal for all dance games, you can play many of these games in smaller spaces. The games that require a large, gymnasium-sized space are marked with the following icon.

Large space needed

Music Where appropriate, suggestions for suitable music are given (see "Choosing the Music" below).

The Structure of Dance Games

Each dance game has an introduction, an exploration, a learning section, and a processing section.

Introduction At the beginning of each dance game, warm up and loosen up the players. Introduce them to the theme of the dance.

Exploration Next, work out the subject or theme of the dance game. Ask the players to work together on the theme and explore particular aspects.

Learning Continue to stress the theme's purpose; encourage players to execute a movement correctly or in a particular way.

Processing When the group has performed the activity fully, draw it to a close by repeating the dances from the earlier part of the session. Or play a restful dance game to allow the participants to wind down and round off the session.

Preparing a Dance Game

The following questions will serve as a useful checklist when you are preparing a session.

- Do I need a tape deck, stereo, or CD player?

- Do I need to make or buy special materials?

- Have I tested the dance game? (Or imagined the outcome of the activity.)

- Do I need to adapt the game in any way?

Here is a list of other points to keep in mind when preparing a dance game.

- Keep other similar dance games in mind in case you need to change the program.

- Ask group members to remove any sharp objects from their pockets and take off rings, earrings, and watches.

- Can the group dance barefoot or is the space not suitable? If players can't go barefoot, ask them to wear gym shoes or ballet shoes. Tight clothing is not advisable; the body must be able to breathe and move freely.

- It may be that you have prepared for a group of thirty and you end up with only fifteen—or vice versa. Be flexible. Dance games with partners in particular may work out differently in such cases.

- Check the play space in advance. Is it clean? Safe? (no sharp corners, splinters in the floor, slippery surfaces, glass partitions, or furniture that could pose a hazard) The floor covering is important: Synthetic indoor-outdoor carpet may be warm, but it can damage the hands and other parts of the body that come into contact with it. A linoleum or hardwood floor is preferable—particularly if the group is barefoot. What is the lighting like? Is it unpleasantly bright? Is there enough fresh air? Is the space noisy? If you have a group of thirty children jumping up and down, will you be disturbing the neighbors? Finally, the acoustics of the space are important: Can your voice and the music be heard from all parts of the room? Are the sounds of the players' movements absorbed by the walls and ceiling?

Time, Length, and Atmosphere

The difference between morning and afternoon for a dance game session is significant. Children are better able to listen in the early morning than late in the afternoon. They are also more wide awake and alert.

Duration of the activity is important, too. With a group of young children, for instance, you can rarely play a game longer than thirty minutes at a time. At that point, many lose interest. If you're planning a session that lasts only five minutes, don't try to work with a complicated dance. Find a dance game that works well as an independent and short activity. Plan a dance game as the last activity of a workshop or time period, or let it take up the entire session.

Remember, too, that a dance game should take place in a relaxed atmosphere. Dance is something you do because you want to; you cannot force someone to dance. If a member of the group doesn't wish to participate, for whatever reason, find an assignment (such as playing the music or holding the props) that allows her or him to not feel left out.

Choosing the Music

The best music for a particular game depends on the role you wish the sound to play:

- to create an atmosphere

- to use as background music

- to guide and support the theme

- to lead the rhythm and tempo of the dance

- to perform or rehearse by

Ask yourself whether music is necessary, for which age group you want to use it, and if music is needed for a few minutes (as a support or for practice) or for longer periods. Sometimes music is necessary as a background; if the members of the group don't know each other yet, silence can make the situation more tense.

Notice that in every piece of music you hear all kinds of instruments and sounds. You might want to follow the sounds of a particular instrument or be carried along by the color of the sound, the rhythm, or the melody to best draw out the theme or movement emphasized in each dance game. Suitable music helps players to feel the movements and enables them to enact your suggestions.

Be aware of your group. Dancing with young children means that you need to choose music with a simple structure. In general, music played on a single instrument is more accessible and easier to understand than multi-instrument ensembles.

Key to the Icons Used in the Games

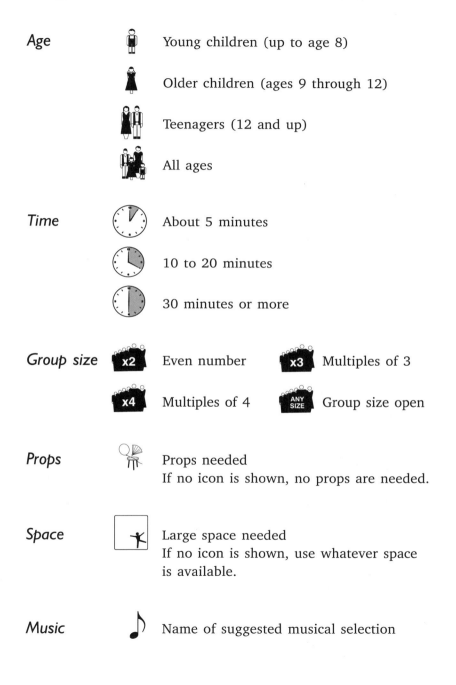

Age   Young children (up to age 8)

Older children (ages 9 through 12)

Teenagers (12 and up)

All ages

Time   About 5 minutes

10 to 20 minutes

30 minutes or more

Group size   **x2** Even number   **x3** Multiples of 3

x4 Multiples of 4   **ANY SIZE** Group size open

Props   Props needed
If no icon is shown, no props are needed.

Space   Large space needed
If no icon is shown, use whatever space
is available.

Music   Name of suggested musical selection

Let's Dance:
Introduction Dances

These games encourage participants to get to know each other better by learning each other's names and coming into contact through dance. In a new group, introductions help to break the ice. These dances loosen up people and lessen their self-consciousness. In these games, avoid situations where the participants watch each other for long periods of time. Have them dance at the same time and come together in different scenarios. These introduction dance games are short and simple, so you can fit them into longer classes.

Dance
of
Names

Ask group members to sit or stand in a circle and say their name in turn. When the last person has said his or her name, have group members repeat their names, going around the circle in the opposite direction. Next, ask each person in the circle to say his or her name again and make a movement at the same time. Ask all the group members to repeat the name and the movement.

Variations:

- Players say their name while stepping forward and doing a movement inside the circle.

- Players divide their name into syllables (Jen-ni-fer, To-ny, Chris-to-pher), take a step forward, and make a new movement for each syllable. Group members repeat the syllables and the movements.

- As above, but this time the group moves around the room while repeating the syllables and movements. The leader claps his hands to indicate the next player's turn, and the group stands still to watch. Then members move around again and imitate the player.

- At your signal (such as two hand-claps), everyone looks for a partner. One partner dances his name and his partner imitates him. In this way, players meet a particular person rather than the whole group. When you clap twice again, players change partners and repeat.

Who Do You Want To Be?

Ask participants to stand in a circle and think of characteristic names for themselves, like Tim the Terrible, Laughing Lisa, or Musical Mary. They can think of a scary name or a cheerful name and put all kinds of feelings into it. The leader can ask the players: How does a Terrible Tim move? What movements would a Paul the Painter make?

To help the group get started, think of a name for yourself and demonstrate a movement to go along with it. Ask a participant what she wants to be and demonstrate a movement for her name. Be ready with a couple of names and movement examples. After one or two examples, participants will usually be able to think of their own names and movements. The participants shouldn't leave the group to think about their names; have them enter into the game spontaneously. As in the last game, have the group constantly mimic each new name and movement, which can, if necessary, be repeated several times.

Variations:

- What mood is each player in? Playful, shy, cheerful, confused? Have players give themselves new names to reflect their mood, then express that name in dance.

- Instead of standing in a circle, have players stand in random places around the room. Just be sure everyone can see the examples.

- Have players sing their chosen names, then dance them.

Character Capers

Have each player find a partner. Ask each pair to think up a set of characters: Mickey Mouse and Minnie Mouse, Aladdin and the Genie. Then give the pairs a few minutes to create a simple dance-step for their characters. Ask each pair to introduce their characters and demonstrate their dance step so that the others can imitate it.

Variations:

- Bring out comic strips or pages from coloring books featuring cartoon and movie characters for inspiration. Have the pairs choose their characters from the pictures.

- Instead of real characters' names, encourage each pair to use aliases or nicknames—but only if they are positive and not hurtful.

- When each pair introduces themselves and dances, have them use a different tone of voice, such as loud for a pirate, soft for a butterfly, or deep for a giant.

Movement Mania

Have the players spread out around the room. Face the group and call out movement words one by one (such as hop, spin, reach, gallop). Have each player do the movement, then keep repeating it. When thinking of movement words, vary the levels at which the players move: such as on the floor, on their feet, on their knees, on tiptoe.

Next, call out five words at once (such as roll, walk, skip, crawl, shuffle). After practicing the five movements, ask each player to choose one movement for herself, which she repeats over and over. After a minute, stop the group and organize everyone by movement: all those who are rolling cluster together, all those who are walking cluster together, and so on.

The smaller groups that form may consist of couples or threes who have not yet worked together and who do not yet know each other.

Ask each small group to choose another movement from the five words. Now each group has two movements. Ask the groups to practice their choice of two movements, agreeing on who follows whom and deciding how many times they will do each movement (for example, one group might do three skips and then two rolls). Ask each group to show their choice of movements to the others.

Variations:

- When calling out the movement words, suggest a different combination, order, and number of repetitions. The participants then dance according to your direction.

- Speed up or slow down the dance tempo. Give a variation, such as slower or faster, for each movement. With adults, add the element of power (more tense or more relaxed movement).

- Play music that stimulates the five movement words. If music is playing, the participants can dance without watching each other so much. Stravinsky's *Firebird* or *The Rite of Spring* are good choices. For small children, a violin or piano solo piece is easier to listen to than an orchestral work.

5

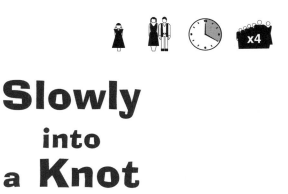

Slowly
into
a **Knot**

Divide the participants into groups of four and choose or ask them to choose one in each group as a leader. Have each group hold hands and stand far enough apart to avoid bumping into another group. At your signal, the leader begins to dance slowly and move the others along. Tell the leaders to move under, between, and over the others until she can go no further and the group has formed a knot. Be sure the leaders dance slowly so that no one's limbs get twisted or hurt. Try this knot dance again with a new group leader.

Variations:

• Choose a slow piece of music, such as Pachelbel's *Canon*.

• Make knots with one partner, two, or even with the whole group of players together.

Hand Dancing

This series begins with simple dance games and continues with more difficult ones. Each dance generally begins with players using their hands and then draws in the whole body. Becoming more conscious of your hands is an important lesson to learn, since losing the use of a finger or hand for a while makes many actions difficult or impossible. Hands are essential to daily life: you use them to wash yourself, eat, write, and work. You use your hands to meet people. Movement and hands are a natural pairing; you might say they go, well, hand in hand!

One Hand

♪ **Music:** slow tempo, solo piano or other instrument

Ask the group to sit in a circle. Slowly demonstrate a movement with your right hand (such as snapping, waving, wiggling fingers) and ask the group to imitate it. Make another movement and repeat it several times. Ask the players to join in and repeat the movement as accurately as possible. Then, switch hands. Demonstrate the same movements with your left hand and ask the players once again to join in and repeat the movement several times. (You'll find that a right hand moves quite differently from a left hand.)

Two Hands

Have the group either sit or stand in a circle. Move both hands in the same way and in the same direction. Have the players copy the movements. Introduce a new movement and have the players follow. Gradually make the movements more difficult. If you see that everyone can follow the pattern easily, change from large gestures to small gestures, or vice versa.

Variations:

• Change the speed of the movements.

• Vary both the size and the speed of one movement. Alter the power of the movement from a very relaxed one to one with great tension.

Mirror Hand Dancing

Pair up the players and ask everyone to stand or sit facing their partner. Ask one person in each pair to start by using one hand to create a series of movements that their partner copies. Then ask the leaders to create movements with both hands, "dancing" their hands in whatever way they wish. Again, their partner follows. After five minutes, the players switch roles. Notice that each player has his own style.

Variations:

- Demonstrate how players can vary the speed, size, and power of the movements.

- Suggest the players get inspiration for their movements from an idea, a story, part of a story, or a fragment of music. Peaceful classical music is suitable for this dance game.

9

All Hands Loose

Ask the group to sit in a circle. Rub your hands together, massaging one hand with the other. Invite participants to rub their hands. Make sure to rub every part of your hand, from wrist to fingertips. While doing so, name the parts of the hand. Warm up both sides of the hands. Then massage each finger, one by one. Shake both hands from the wrist up and down, down and up, from side to side and finally, wave at someone in the group.

10

Body
and
Limbs

♪ **Music:** A slow piece of classical music

Moving just your hands is difficult. Usually, the lower part of your arm begins to move spontaneously and, before you know it, you're dancing. Your joints play an important role in this process. The arm becomes involved when the hand moves. The hand brings the arm, shoulder, head, and upper body into the dance.

Have players stand in a circle and imitate your movements. Start by moving just your hands, keeping your arms still. Tell the players to concentrate and keep their arms as still as possible. Next, slowly move your hands and arms. Add your shoulder and head to the movement. Gradually increase the degree of difficulty in the movement, until you finally add leg movements. Try to show a constantly changing flow of movements in the upper body.

Ask each player to choose a partner and together make up a series of slow movements. After a few minutes of practice, have each pair demonstrate their dance improvisation.

Mirroring Your Hands

♪ **Music:** slow tempo music

Ask players to form pairs, choose a leader, and find a space in the room. The leaders move gently and freely to the music, and their partner moves as their mirror image. Tell the leaders to choose simple, slow movements to begin with because their partner has to do the opposite; whatever the leaders do with the right hand is mirrored by their partner's left. After a while, have the partners switch roles.

If the leaders need help thinking of hand movements, tell them to start with ones they make every day. Ask them: What are the first ten movements you make with your hands when you get up in the morning? When you eat? When you get to school?

Variation: Have the leaders use upper body and leg movements instead of hand movements.

Painting
with
Your Hands

♪ **Music:** fast and rhythmic music

This dance game is more flexible than "Mirroring Your Hands." Ask each player to find a space in the room and pretend that one hand holds a paintbrush. On your signal, ask everyone to begin to use their paintbrush and paint in the air. Tell players it doesn't matter if they go "outside the lines." Encourage everyone to follow the music and move around the room, using larger and larger painting movements. Let them use their imagination to paint large murals with broad strokes, and dance the performance of their painting.

Variation: Ask players to form pairs and work on one painting together.

This
and
That

This dance game—which is a variation of "Simon Says"—begins simply with the hands, but you can build it up to include the whole body.

Have the players face you. Demonstrate a movement with your hand. If you say "this" while making the movement, the players should also make the movement. If you say "that" while making the movement, the players should remain still. Keep making hand movements, calling out either "this" or "that."

Use this game as a warm-up or to form groups: anyone who is "out" for making a wrong movement can, for instance, team up with the next person to be out, and they can begin again.

Variations:

- Create a series of movements using your whole body and ask players to imitate them—but only if you say "this."

- Once the players imitate a movement, have them freeze. You can then see if anyone has made a wrong movement.

A **Hallway** of **Hands**

♪ **Music:** slow synthesizer music

Ask players to stand in two lines and face each other, with about three feet between them. These two lines of players create a "hallway." Start the music and encourage the players to slowly stretch out their hands toward each other, but without touching. There's no prearranged movement, although you can make one if you want. Ask some players to kneel and others to sit so that the hands can come from above or below, toward the center.

At your signal, have the players begin to dance using their entire bodies, not just their hands. Ask one player to break out and dance down the center of the two lines. When he reaches

the end of the line, let another player dance down the center, and so on, until all the players have had a turn.

Variations:

- The "wall people" can gently capture the player in the center and then let him go.

- Incorporate a story about a hallway into the dance game.

Let Your Hand Lead

♪ **Music:** lively classical guitar music

Divide the group into pairs and ask each pair to find a starting point somewhere in the room. Have them agree who will be the leader and who will be the follower. Start the music and tell the leaders to take the hand of the followers and dance them around the room: up high, down low, over nonexistent obstacles, through valleys, and over mountains. The leaders' fantasy drives the dance. The follower can let go of the leader if necessary but should try to improvise with the same speed and power. After a while, have the pairs switch roles.

Variations:

- Ask the partners not to hold hands, but keep their hands close, almost touching. Have them try to keep their hands at this close distance while continuing to dance.

- Ask the followers to connect a part of their body, such as their elbow or head, with the leaders' hand. Although the dancers can't actually hold on to each other, tell the leaders to lead the followers by that part of their body.

- Have the dancers lead themselves around the room by "pushing" a part of their body away with their hand. For example, have them push their hand against their shoulder to turn and lead their body into the room. Or have them push their hand against their stomach to dance their body backward. This pushing can even be a light slap or tap; have the dancers propel themselves around the room by touching or tapping a different part of their bodies each time.

- With an experienced group, pairs of dancers can turn this game into an imitation fight. Have one player propel the other around the room, almost touching her with her hands.

Meeting Dances

In daily life, meeting people is quite common, but for some of us it can be uncomfortable. What do you do when you meet someone? What is your attitude? The first meeting often determines the development of the acquaintance. You can meet a person, but you can also try to avoid him. In a dance, you always meet other people. Seeking, making, and building up contact is the basis of these games.

16

Sudden Meetings

♪ **Music:** instrumental music with strongly contrasting rhythms

Ask the players to spread themselves around the room. Give a signal and call out three contrasting movement words, such as hop, skate, and dash. (*Skating* means making large gliding movements with the arms and legs; *dashing* means darting from one spot to another.) Have the players choose a movement and dance around in this way for a few minutes. Let them get used to the movement and to the fact that they keep meeting up with other people. Then change to three new movement words.

Variations:

• Players can make the movements alternately high and low.

• When players meet another player, have them freeze in position for a count of three.

• Don't tell the players when to change movements; let them decide for themselves.

• Tell the players that if one of them stops when passing another, the second player must also freeze in position. Let the players decide when to stop or not stop.

Meeting
and Avoiding

♪ **Music:** pop or film music with contrast

Have each player find a partner, spread around the room, and stand facing each other. Have them dance around each other, letting their hands steer them. Tell them that they can encircle their partner with their gestures, go over and under each other, or dart their hands between the other's arms—but they should not touch. They can also make the movements more complete, dancing around each other with their whole bodies, skimming past. Throughout this game, however, the partners must try to avoid touching.

Variations:

• Combine this with dance game 16, "Sudden Meetings."

• Have players dance around the room without partners. When they meet someone, have them dance around the other player and try to come as close as they can to each other, but at the last moment have them avoid each other.

• Have players dance around the room without partners. When they meet someone, have them gently touch the other's shoulders, elbows, and knees. Then have them dash away across the room and search for another player to meet.

• Have each player begin in his own place in the room. Give a signal and have everyone drift away to another spot. If a player meets up with someone, the two players should come close then suddenly try to avoid each other, throwing their bodies in opposite directions and immediately drifting away again.

Meeting
and
Passing by

♪ **Music:** electronic music or classical ballet music

Ask players to spread around the room. Suggest a few stimulating movement words such as "forging ahead" or "held back by a strong wind." Have each player choose a spot on the opposite side of the room and keep an eye on it as a destination. At your signal the players start to move to that spot. They should avoid other players but find the shortest route to their chosen place. If they will run into someone else, they should get out of each other's way just in the nick of time. Be aware that this game can be dangerous. If necessary, let half of the group play the game while the others watch, then swap places. Players should dance high and low with plenty of power.

Variation: Have players listen for the moments in the music that inspire them to move forward, backward, or to the side, and have them react accordingly.

The Swan Joins the Flock

♪ **Music:** light piano music

Have the players find a space in the room. Face them and encourage them to imitate you as you show the elegant steps of the swan: making themselves very large, flying away, and gliding down onto the water. After they have done the steps in one place, encourage them to fly around the room, then glide, then make themselves small and large. Continue to call out the movements.

As players meet others, have them hold hands or touch shoulders and try to continue to perform the movements while holding onto one another.

Drifting
Leaves,
Growing
Trees

♪ **Music:** electronic music

Begin this dance with no music. Have everyone hop around the room in a very relaxed way—arms and legs should swing around loosely. When players meet up with someone, have them stop for a moment and attach themselves to the other person with their arms or legs. Then have them release and continue hopping. After several similar encounters, pick two players and have them hold hands or attach elbows or shoulders together. The tree is born.

Play the music and have the movement change; everyone should be relaxed, like leaves that are wafting upward and looking for a way back to the tree. Show the players how silently the wind lifts a leaf and how the leaf drifts and falls. The tree continues to move through the room. Because of the movement, the tree is visible, just as the leaves are. Eventually, have each player (leaf) join the tree. When the tree is full the action ceases. Vary the movement (fast, slow) and the pace of the meetings.

21

Spaghetti
and Pudding

♪ **Music:** slow classical ballet music

Without music, ask the players to stand in place. Then have them throw themselves into the air and flop down, very relaxed. As players jump up, have them breathe in. As they flop down, have them breathe out. Visual images may help them jump up and flop down: tell them their bodies are like wobbly pudding that always collapses, or like spaghetti sliding out of the pan. Have them do these movements several times, each time in a new way. Then start the music and have the players do the same exercise, but now at random around the room. Make sure they don't touch or bump into anyone else.

Finally, have players choose partners with whom they can have pudding and spaghetti meetings: have them lean against each other, slide over each other, and try to get up together but without holding each other.

Variations:

- Have the dancers show their partner one or two pudding shapes in dance, or how spaghetti looks in dance.

- Encourage dancers to listen to a piece of music and shape their pudding or spaghetti movements according to how the music develops.

Communication Dance

♪ **Music:** peaceful synthesizer music

Have players choose partners and stand opposite each other with eyes closed. Make sure there is enough space around each pair so that no one will bump into anyone. Have the partners place their fingertips together. Start the music and tell the partners to slowly move their fingers and hands as if communicating with each other. Have each pair remain more or less in the same spot and make sure players don't lose their balance. After the game, have the players tell their partners what they were trying to communicate through their finger and hand movements.

Variations:

- At the beginning of the game, have players stand with their eyes closed and put people together in pairs. Pick one person out of each pair to open her eyes and act as leader. Tell leaders to lead their partner around the room, dancing with him, and making sure that he doesn't bump into anything. Use a slow tempo. Ask each dancer: What do you want to communicate to your partner?

- Have partners stand back to back with their eyes closed for a dance called "Back Talk." Ask the dancers: What can you communicate to each other with your backs?

 **23**

Secretly in Pursuit

♪ **Music:** up-tempo classical music

Ask each player to take a spot in the room and make sure everyone has enough space around them so that they can move about quickly. Demonstrate some movements and have the players imitate you: dance like a fish in a fast-running stream, swept along in the swift current; dance like a seed being blown in the air by the wind; or dance like a pebble being tossed on the shore by ocean waves. Now tell the players to think of a person in the group that they want to pursue and make close contact with. Start the music and let the imaginary stream, wind, or ocean waves carry the players around the room. Without the other person being aware of it, players dance to within a few inches of their chosen person. That person should have no idea that someone is trying to approach her. It is much more fun to find out later whether or not one player knew she was being followed. Dancers repeat this a few times, then pursue someone else. Dancers come to realize that someone may also be following them, too.

King
for
a Day

🎵 **Music:** up-tempo classical music

Have dancers stand in their own place and ask them to slowly bend and stretch, not only straight down but in all directions—to the front, to the back, sideways—right down to the ground. Alternate this with stretching up and making the body as big as possible, also in every direction. Exhale with each movement; tell the dancers to bend or stretch as long as possible until they have to take a breath. Then breathe in and make the next movement.

After several minutes, have the players move around the room, bending and stretching. Have them stretch out grandly, as if they are regal. Then have them bow humbly, as if they are subservient. Practice both movements to music while dancing around the room.

Now, give everyone a chance to be "king for a day." Choose one player to dance like the king while the others dance around him like subjects. Ask them: How does a king dance? How does a subject dance? Point out the possibilities of being a cheerful, cruel, or disconsolate ruler, for instance, and a clever, foolish, or kind subject. Make sure everyone has a chance to dance the role of the king.

Dancing Feet

♪ **Music:** classical ballet music

Spread the players around the room. Start the music and encourage the players to dance around the room, making steps in as many different ways as possible: feet close together, far apart, heavy, wide paces, light elfin tiptoes that don't make a sound, and so on. Call out a number of ideas during the dance: Place your feet quickly and lightly; sideways; next to you; in front of you; in all directions; heavy, large, slow; constantly changing speed, power, and direction. Have the dancers pair off and continue, dancing around each other. Have them make a dance of about thirty seconds to show to each other.

Variation: Have the group watch the movie *The Red Shoes* (1948), which is based on a Hans Christian Andersen fairy tale. Play this dance game after the movie.

Cooperation Dances

Cooperation is an essential element of dance: dancers seldom dance alone, and they are usually on the dance floor with other dancers. Cooperation also means working together. This section includes warming-up exercises that players do with a partner and from which a dance game is developed. You can use the following games to prepare for other dance games. These dance games are not meant to be a part of technical dance training, although some are physically challenging. Introduce these games in a relaxed but careful way.

26

Loosening Up

Ask each player to choose a spot in the room and keep their hands loose or make a relaxed fist. Then have them gently "drum" their bodies loose. Using soft and rhythmic motions, ask them to pat their head. Then move behind the head and on down the neck. Drum with one hand on the opposite shoulder, then the other hand on the other shoulder. Have players drum on their back with both hands from the top downward. At the kidneys, have players drum very softly but a little longer. Then have them slap their buttocks with their hands held flat or loose.

Now have the players sit down and raise one leg. Ask them to drum along the underside of their leg, touching the calves with one hand at a time, not both together. Have them lay the leg on the ground and drum down the front of it, from the torso downward. Do the same with the other leg.

Have everyone stand up again and begin drumming down their front from the top downward. Drum gently around the tummy area; around the torso, drum a little longer with hands closed in a fist. Finally, have players shake their arms loose and let their whole body wiggle while they bounce loosely up and down on their toes. Have them uncurl their feet as much as possible.

Variation: Players can also loosen each other up by "walking" along the other's body with loose, relaxed hands. Or, they can loosen up their partner by taking first her hands, then feet, and gently wiggling her partner's limbs.

Chairs
in the Air

Ask players to practice sitting on an imaginary chair and then standing up. Encourage them to keep their arms stretched out in front, their heels on the floor, and their legs together. When players have mastered this technique, have them sit on the imaginary chair in different ways (for example, putting one leg to the side and one arm in the air). In between each new position, have the players stand up for a moment and exhale deeply.

Ask each player to find a partner and try to sit on each other's knees. This is impossible if the players keep their legs together (and it's not healthy for the knees either). Have the partners experiment to find a position where sitting on each other's knees is possible (for example, putting one leg a little in front).

Now ask the group to stand in a circle facing the back of the person in front of them. At your signal, have everyone slowly sit down, so that the players end up on each other's knees. Can the whole group remain sitting like this?

Rolling Carpet

Have participants lie down on their stomachs on a clean floor, with their arms stretched out above their heads, parallel and close to one another. Ask them to keep their body as relaxed as possible. Now ask one player to lie down on top of the first person at one end of the "carpet," keeping his arms out-stretched. At your signal, have everyone roll in one direction and the player on the top rolls in the other direction until he gradually rolls down the whole length of the carpet and off the other end, at which point he becomes part of the carpet. Now the next player in line can lay on top of the carpet and roll off the other end. Continue rolling until everyone has had a turn to be on top, changing the directions of the rolls to accommodate the size of the room.

Variations:

- Have a player roll over the carpet, while the others remain still.

- Ask the players on the floor to keep their arms by their sides and the person rolling to lie sideways across the first three people, on his stomach. Now the players on the floor can roll him along as if on a conveyor belt.

Stretching
and
Bending

Ask players to sit on the floor in pairs, back to back, with their elbows linked together and their knees bent. Ask them to breathe out as together they move up to a standing position. Then have them sit down again, back to back, this time with their legs stretched out in front and their arms hanging loose on the floor. Ask them to push each other up without using their hands, again exhaling.

Next, have partners sit facing each other, toes touching. They hold each other by their wrists and pull each other up slowly while exhaling. Then they bend and sit down again.

Encourage players to complete these exercises slowly while exhaling, and to stretch and bend only as far as is comfortable.

The
Obstacle
Course

Have everyone get down on their hands and knees and form a circle, keeping about ten inches apart from each other. One player starts, moving around the circle, using only her arms to move in only one direction and in one way: over the back of the first person, under the next person, over the third person, and so on. She continues to pull herself up over one player, then slide off and under the next, until she completes the circle. Let everyone have a turn maneuvering through this obstacle course.

Balance

♪ **Music:** up-tempo piano music

Players stand in pairs facing each other, holding their hands stretched out in front, touching their partner. The game begins simply: one of the partners stretches out while the other assists him. The pairs' hands remain pressed together as one stretches in all kinds of positions: up high, lower, and down close to the ground. The player who is not stretching should stand in such a way that he cannot fall over (for example, keeping the knees bent and one foot slightly in front of the other). Partners then change roles. Have the partners stretch and balance in a gentle, continuous tempo.

Now, ask players to try to dance their partners off balance. One partner flows along with what the other does and tries to make fluid bends, corners, and lines with her arms and those of her partner.

32

The Resistance Walk

Have players choose partners and warm up together. Encourage everyone to stretch out slowly; the idea is to stretch the stomach and back muscles gently. One partner can stretch out first by holding onto her partner by the wrists and putting her foot sideways against one of her partner's feet. Have each partner stretch out in various ways and directions, while the other assists.

Now have all the pairs stand in one corner of the room and each pair choose a leader and a resister. The resister sits on her haunches, one leg slightly in front of the other, and holds onto the leader with both hands just above the knees. The leader tries to move to the other side of the room. She stretches, breathes out, and tries to move forward as the resister holds on. When all pairs have crossed the room, the partners change places and cross the room again.

The
Circle

Divide the class into small groups. Have each group hold hands and form a circle with one player standing in the center. Slowly and with great care, the circle moves in and pushes the person in the middle to the other side of the circle and back again. The player in the center keeps his eyes open and allows the others to move him first one way, then another, which relaxes him more and more. He can hold his hands out in front so as not to bump into the others. Encourage him to turn in the circle. The people in the circle should stand with legs apart and knees slightly bent so as to be stable enough to catch and propel the person in the center. The players do this to-ing and fro-ing more and more quickly.

Ask the circle to spread out a little. Now, the player in the middle becomes the center of the circle, and must keep at least one foot on the center spot. Without touching the others, he makes long, short, quick movements toward them while they, in turn, try to dance him away from his place. Since this dance game does not involve touching, it allows the players to make beautiful movements as they reach and move quickly. Encourage players to stretch in all directions from their spots.

After a few minutes, choose someone else to go in the middle and begin again.

The
Bridge

♪ **Music:** very slow, meditative piano music

Stand players in pairs facing each other with their legs apart and their arms stretched out in front. Have them take each other by the arms and bend their upper bodies forward, keeping their arms stretched out. Then have them braid their arms over and under each other. Their heads should hang down loose and they should lean forward, keeping their legs straight. Now have them move their torsos gently so that together they form a hanging bridge that swings gently back and forth. ("Swinging" means a small movement, but one that players can feel. Take care!)

Think up another form players can make together in which they can flow, bend, and stretch (for example, a hammock or a tire swing). Encourage players to make one form flow into the next. Don't think about what should be done next. Show the bending and stretching movements in a new dance game.

On
the
Back

Ask players to form pairs and find a space in the room. One partner gets down on her hands and knees. The other partner drapes herself forward across the other's back, totally relaxed and loose. She should hang carefully and not force any movements by herself or her partner. Slowly, the carrier moves around the room, with her partner on her back like a sack of flour. (Players with weak knees or backs should not attempt this game.) Players then change places and repeat.

Have the group form threes. Ask two people to get down on their hands and knees and carry the third on their backs. The two carriers shouldn't be too far apart; the person on top should first lie on her front, then lie on her back. The two carriers must start and stop at the same time, and should crawl slowly and carefully. Keep a watchful eye on the proceedings.

Dancing with Props

The use of materials or inspiration from a particular prop is central to the dance games in this section. Players can, for example, dance with paper, cloth, plastic, elastic, string, boxes, balloons, fans, sticks, ribbons, newspapers, and balls. Or they can dance without props but still describe a particular material or thing: players can dance as a metal robot, a wooden doll, or a leaf blowing in the wind. Players are guided by how the materials behave if they are picked up, thrown in the air, or rolled on the ground. You'll find ways of dancing with material—in reality and in fantasy—in these next few games.

36

The
Fan Dance

Materials: fans, either made from paper or store-bought

♪ **Music:** quiet but exciting film music

Have players make themselves as small as possible and cover their body with their hands. Of course, they won't be able to cover their entire body at one time, but they should cover what they want. With a group of small children, call out the parts of the body that they should cover: ears, eyes, cover one leg with the other, or roll into a ball.

Have the players move around in pairs, covering each other and showing as little as possible. Ask the players: Are you now both invisible? As the partners try to cover each other, they will produce some nice shapes.

Now give one or two fans to each player and play the music. Ask the players to dance around the room covering themselves in different ways. Encourage them to hide, then reappear. Give directions to use different levels of tempo, power, and space.

Variations:

- Have the players improvise with different partners or make up a dance in a small group and perform it in front of the rest of the group.

- Have dancers pretend that the wind is blowing them and their fan. Encourage them to change direction, just as the fan chooses a new direction during the dance. Have the dancers wave the fan in the air, throw their bodies after it, turn with the fan upward, then downward, then wave each other away with the fan. Have the fans give their body wings.

"Around the Corner..."

Materials: furniture, such as chairs, large and small tables, and stools

♪ **Music:** music with a changing tempo

"Around the corner, life is different"...this dance game communicates this expression. We don't know what is around the corner. Is it nice; is it scary?

Arrange the furniture in the room in an unusual way. For example, put the chairs upside down, bunch all the tables together, or ask the group to arrange the furniture as if there has been an earthquake. Ask the players to dance around the furniture, peering over chairs and table tops, searching under cushions, or looking over the pile for what is around the corner. Have the players dance what they find.

38

Fossils Coming to Life

Materials: a few fossils

♪ **Music:** exciting film music

Show the group a few fossils and explain how they were formed. Then ask the players to spread around the room and tell them that they have turned to stone and have to work themselves loose. Have them start in a frozen position. Encourage them to turn their head, eyes, and neck; pull their faces; rotate their shoulders, arms, elbows, wrists, and fingers; massage their face with their hands; pummel their body (as in dance game 26, "Loosening Up"). Have them shake and pummel every part of themselves and slowly move their awakened body, first stretching out, then making themselves as small as they can. They can shrink and expand, first on the spot and then as they move around the room. Let the players try these moves for a while.

Ask the players to stretch out on the ground and slowly shrink again using variations in speed and power. Have dancers choose different places in the room to turn to stone in one shape after another, and from the ground, dance like animated fossils. Have players show which part can no longer move.

Now tell players that they are only able to move along the floor. Tell them to lie flat on the ground and pretend to stick to other pieces of stone, fossils, or blocks of ice. Since fossils can be stuck with various parts of the body fossilized, have dancers show if they are stuck to the floor by their bottom, head, feet, back, or in some other way.

Finally, in groups of about four have them demonstrate to the rest of the group how fossils can come to life.

Under
and
Over Sheets

Materials: a double-sized sheet for each participant. With small children, use a large sweater or overcoat.

♪ **Music:** synthesizer or slow classical music

Let the players practice looking at and playing with the sheet. Encourage them to put the sheet on the ground and make pleats and shapes with it. Have them drape the sheet around themselves in different ways.

Have players lay their sheet down again and become an extension of it by staying on top, underneath, partly underneath, or above it.

Ask players to spread out their sheets again. At a signal from you, players make a journey from one sheet to the next, dancing around the room and taking up a different posture on or under each sheet for a few seconds.

Have players improvise a dance on their own sheet in any way they like, as long as they don't step off the edge of the sheet. Have them try the same thing under the sheet: players can make whatever movements they can think of, as long as they cannot be seen. Have them move about with the sheet, but remain invisible.

Variation: Separate players into groups of four and have them invent a dance using their sheets. Ask them to show their dance to the group.

Plastic Play

Materials: a piece of nontransparent agricultural plastic, approximately 15 x 30 feet, or a parachute

♪ **Music:** slow, heavy electronic music

Have the players space themselves out evenly along the plastic, and grab hold of the edge of the plastic with one hand. The plastic should be stretched somewhat taut. Show the players how, by raising and lowering their hands, they can make the plastic ripple.

Have the players begin to dance slowly, rippling the plastic. Then, have them dance toward the center, winding themselves up in the plastic until they come together in a knot. When they become too tangled to dance, have the players gradually unwind, until they are dancing free of the plastic again.

Make sure to remind the players not to handle the material too roughly or it will tear.

Next, have everyone stretch the plastic so it is taut like a trampoline. Show the players how to "bounce" it up and down by lifting the plastic up then pulling it down at the same time. While bouncing the plastic, have players run one-by-one under the plastic.

Variations:

- Throw the plastic in the air and let half the group dart or dance underneath the plastic.

- Several people together can throw the material in the air and dance under it from one side to the other, without touching the plastic.

Being a Balloon

Materials: a large balloon for each player—and a few extras in case some pop

♪ **Music:** slow, new-age piano music

Blow up a balloon and let it deflate, either by holding it open or letting it fly around the room. Give each participant a balloon and have them blow up and deflate their balloons a few times. Inflate the balloons one more time and tie them shut. Put them aside for a moment.

Dance the movements of blowing up and deflating. Have each player stand in one spot and, on your signal, dance the inflation and deflation by pumping themselves up, then letting the air out. Then have the players pump up and deflate themselves as they move around the room. Divide the group in two and let one group watch the others. Encourage players to use high and low movements: for example, players could let themselves deflate as they wriggle across the floor.

Form pairs and let each partner pump the other up and let him deflate. Have the pumping partner dance along behind the deflating partner. Then change roles.

Ask everyone to take a balloon and dance in one spot with it, holding it in the air. Encourage dancers to make all sorts of silly movements. Tell them to move around the room and to watch the other players' balloons. Tell them to move with the balloon under their arm, between their legs, clasped against their chest, and so on. Have them dance with the balloon while holding it, sometimes changing the way they hold it. Have the players see if they can move around on the floor while holding their balloon.

Finally, separate the players into groups of about four and have them invent a dance in which the balloon plays an important role. After a few minutes, have the small groups perform their dance for the others.

42

Moving In and Out of Boxes

Materials: a large cardboard box for each participant—and a few extra in case some get broken during the dancing; a couple of large flashlights

♪ **Music:** mysterious music in a variety of tempos

Keep the boxes on one side of the room. Ask the players to approach an imaginary stack of boxes and, in mime, pick up a box and put it down somewhere in the room. Have everyone make themselves small, climb into their imaginary box, close the box, and wait for the music to start. Play the music and call out a part of the body. Have players slowly move out of the box, stretching out that part of their body first, and then pulling back in again. Have the players try leaving the box from different starting positions and letting different parts of their bodies appear first from the box.

After this make-believe round, let players pick a real box and place it on the ground. Repeat the instructions with the real box. Ask the players: How do you dance out of the box? Are you happy or sad? Can you walk or do you roll along like an animal? Ask players to move in and out of their box several times, trying out different positions and moods each time.

Form small groups and make up a dance in which the box plays an important part. After a few minutes, have the small groups perform these short dance improvisations for the rest of the group.

43

Elastic Movements

Materials: 3 to 6 feet of elastic for each person

♪ **Music:** slow, mysterious film music

Use the following three exercises to warm up the group.

First, play a statue game: twirl the players and, when you call out "statue," have them freeze in whatever position they find themselves.

Second, twirl the players again, but this time tell them that they have some elasticity; as they move, they can stretch out in all directions.

Third, have pairs form a boomerang. Ask one player to twirl her partner; the boomerang moves in an arc and comes back to where she started—being sure not to bump into anyone else on the way. As she flies, she moves in every direction, high and low. Make sure each partner gets a chance to be the boomerang.

Now hand out the elastic and encourage the players to experiment and see how they can stretch in every direction. Tell them to keep the elastic extended and straight. Have them dance around the room with the elastic; along the ground and up in the air. Play music and have players follow the tempo.

Ask the group to form pairs. Have them hold their elastic strips and step inside them, keeping the strips tight while both partners try stretching themselves. Have the pairs move around, high and low, in time to the music. Ask the pairs to invent a dance that they can perform after a few minutes of practice.

44

Taut and Loose Ribbons

Materials: a rolled-up ball made up of long lengths of ribbon; a separate piece of ribbon, about a yard long, for each player

♪ **Music:** slow synthesizer music

Have the players form a circle and give the ball of ribbon to one of the participants. Ask that person to hold the end of the ribbon, call out someone's name, and throw him the ball of ribbon. Now have that person hold onto a part of the ribbon, call out someone else's name, and throw him the ball. Continue throwing the ball until a web is made and everyone's name has been called several times. (This activity also makes a good introduction game.)

Now ask the players to roll up the ribbon again while dancing high and low. They should try to avoid bumping into each other while doing so.

Next, give the players a piece of ribbon each and ask them to hold the ribbon stretched tightly (for example, with one end under their foot and the other in their hand). Encourage them to find as many ways as possible to stretch out while keeping their ribbon taut, and to bend and relax while letting the ribbon hang loose. Have each player try this while lying on the floor.

Form pairs and have the couples stretch out while keeping their two ribbons taut. Have them move around the room together, high and low.

Next, ask half of the group to stay in one position, with ribbons taut or loose, standing or lying down. Have the others dance without ribbons, around, along, perhaps over the ribbons, and try out all kinds of movements.

Variations: Introduce the idea of electricity: the ribbons are electrified. When two players touch their ribbons, they receive a burst of electricity and can "shoot off" in different directions. Encourage the players to use their full imaginations to make a dance with the electrified ribbons and demonstrate the dance for the others.

Toilet Paper Webs

Materials: several rolls of toilet paper

♪ **Music:** exciting film music

Create groups of threes and give each group about fifteen feet of toilet paper. Ask two of the players to hold the paper stretched out straight, but not on the same spot or at the same level. Have the third member dance over and under the paper while the other members move the paper around. Have the members dare each other to make extra movements. The two holding the paper can dance as well but they must remain in

the same spot, otherwise the groups will become mixed up. Tell the members to dance carefully because the paper can easily be torn. And remind the players holding the paper not to pull on it so it doesn't tear.

Ask the players to vary the speed with which they make the movements and form the lines. Have them change places within their group so that everyone has a chance to dance solo.

Variations:

- Have the players create a large web around the room by holding the paper while standing in different parts of the room. Form pairs. Have pairs of players lead each other through the web. Ask one partner to keep her eyes closed while the other leads her through. Remind the players that the web feels larger when you cannot see.

- Ask groups of about four to make a dance to music using the strands of toilet paper.

Imagination Dances

The following series of dance games develops the power of imagination and feeling, essential elements of dance. The scope of feeling possible in dance is immeasurable, and these ten dance games touch only the tip of the iceberg. You will find that basic dramatic forms have been adapted to these games, and many more can be thought up on the same basis. Realize that working with feelings may create tension. Not everyone finds it easy to express themselves, and dancing may cause new feelings to surface.

Living Statues

This dance game has its origin in the game *tableaux vivants* (living paintings), where a group represents a particular scene by remaining frozen in a portrait.

Separate the large group into groups of four people each. Ask each group to think of a mood or feeling (such as joy or sadness) and a way to represent that mood or feeling in a stationary position. Give each group time to practice. Ask each group to form its tableau and let the others guess what the group is representing.

Now ask the groups to think of an action or situation (for example, bicycling or mowing the lawn). After each group has had time to practice, have them show their tableau to the rest of the group. Let the group guess the situation.

Finally, ask each group to portray a series of five situations. Tell them they must move without speaking from one tableau to the next, holding each pose for a moment but completing the whole series before stopping.

Variations: Try dance games 92, "Slowly Moving Scenes," and 93, "The Photo Album."

Creating Characters

Ask each player to choose a character to dance: for example, a cantankerous person, a happy-go-lucky, a lazy-bones, a sinister character, or an indifferent person. Ask each player how his character moves, walks, sits, picks things up, drops things, meets other people, and gestures. Suggest repeating or exaggerating some typical movements so that the dancer quickly reveals characteristics: someone who is sad becomes sadder and sadder until she is weeping or sobbing.

Have each player choose a partner and show a succession of portrayals of their chosen character to him, as if in a short, thirty-second film. Each movement should flow into the next. Ask partners to make comments and suggest improvements.

Finally, ask each player to choose two other characters in the room that match their original character (or that are completely the opposite). Ask them to perform a dance with these three characters in which the characters show their feelings to each other.

This dance game can be adapted for different age groups.

The Feeling Machine

♪ **Music:** circus music or cartoon film music, in a variety of tempos

Ask players to choose a favorite feeling to portray to the group. Now ask the participants to think of a sequence of feelings. Ask the players: Which feelings belong after each other? Which ones give rise to which? For example, a happy feeling might follow a sad one; a puzzled feeling might give rise to one of understanding.

Make sure that the players dance and do not speak. Inspire the players to vary the height, breadth, speed, and power with which they move.

Variation: With a small group, have each player become a "feeling machine," which portrays all sorts of feelings one after another, with movements that go with each one.

Dance
of the Dolls

♪ **Music:** a fragment recorded from a toy, music box, or computer game, medium tempo

Describe different kinds of dolls and have players dance them:

- a wooden doll, who dances stiffly

- a tin soldier, who dances angularly and can hardly bend

- a rag doll, who cannot stand up and keeps rolling in an attempt to sit up straight.

After dancing several such examples, ask players to choose their favorites. Ask the players: Would you prefer to be a floppy doll or a stiff one? What kind of dance would dolls make if they came to life? What kinds of characteristics would they have?

Remind players that their facial expressions must remain the same. Let the participants tell the group what characters they are going to develop, then sort them into groups based on the type of doll they want to be. Have everyone dance, first in groups and then all together.

50

ANY SIZE

The Language of Gesture

Have the players find a space in the room. Call out several actions that the players can do without preparation:

- welcoming someone

- clapping your hands

- waving to a friend across the street

- begging forgiveness

- yelling "Scram!"

- saying, "Ssshhh, I can hear something . . . ."

Have the players attach a movement or series of movements to each action. Call out these gestures again but now say them faster or slower. Tell players to act out these gestures while on the floor, running, walking around, and rolling. Choose gestures that change their context when they are danced.

Form small groups. Ask each group to make a series of five gestures. Have them repeat the gestures in different ways: high and low, together, alone, and with a propelling movement. Ask the groups to show the dance to the rest of the group. Can everyone still recognize the different gestures? Make sure that the group clearly shows the accompanying emotion and that the emotion changes with each gesture.

Creeping
Happily
and Running
Sadly

Ask the players to spread around the room and dance a series of feelings you call out. Ask them to dance happily, fearfully, disappointedly, ecstatically (such as when you've just won a prize), miserably.

Have the players dance these feelings while staying in one spot and then while moving around the room. Ask them to choose a particular feeling and dance it on their toes, then while bending over to avoid low branches, and then while rolling along the ground. Can players still dance the emotion in these different positions? Ask them to dance the emotion while running, creeping, struggling, skating, and then swinging. Call out a new movement word only when everyone has the hang of the last movement.

Ask half of the group to watch while the other half demonstrates the series of movements you suggest. Repeat the movement words. Then ask groups to switch places and call out other movement words. Form groups of four. Ask each group to create a dance featuring four emotions. Encourage the groups to enact the emotions using unusual combinations. For example, running and fear go together, but suggest to each group to show fear and painting or fear and eating cake. Make some unusual combinations.

The
Scary Movie

♪ **Music:** fragments of scary or tension-building music

As a warm-up, start the music and have participants practice a number of tense movement words and emotions, such as:

- standing fixed to the spot in terror

- trembling and shaking with rage

- shuddering with fear and making themselves small

- skulking and creeping away in fear

- coming to the edge of an abyss but without fear

- shocked, jumping in the air

- cautious and quiet as a tiger, creeping, on their toes

Form groups of four. Play a short piece of music, 20 to 30 seconds long, which sets the scene for each group's dance or "scary movie." What movements combined with which emotions can each group hear in the musical fragment?

Have the groups practice the movements in an agreed order, then let them play their music and perform for the rest of the group.

War
and
Peace

♪ **Music:** up-tempo classical music

Warm up the players by practicing a number of quick, tense, and abrupt movements. No real conflict should be going on in the group, as this could make the dancing impossible. Don't mention the theme of the game yet: bring the players into the right mood simply through the warm-up instructions.

Ask each player to find a space in the room. Tell them that they suddenly feel drawn to another spot in the room. Have them quickly rush across the room to the new spot, but once they arrive they are pushed away, their bodies are pushed back, both high and low, by some invisible force.

Next, form pairs and have the partners practice a mock fight. Instruct the participants that they must never actually touch. As a player reaches out to hit his partner, he is repelled. Let this go on back and forth first with pairs "fighting," then with small groups making "war." Now have them do this to music.

Now, ask the groups of four to make up a dance to music in which they create their own gestures for making "peace" with another group. Have the other players observe each group's "peace" dance.

54

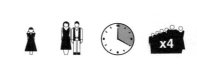

Dance
Cards I

Materials: dance cards made from paper, about three inches square

Create the dance cards before the session, or, if you like, have group members create the cards during the session. On each card, write, draw, or attach a photograph that describes a feeling (such as happy), a movement (jump), a space (on the spot, around the room, or from corner to corner), a tempo (quickly, slowly, jerkily), and an indication of power (relaxed or with clenched fists). These are all states in which the players will dance.

Give each player a card and allow them time to practice the instructions. Ask each player to perform without saying a word. If they pass in front of someone, that person can guess what the player is doing. If the person guesses correctly, they form a couple.

Form groups of four and tell players to make a dance using the ideas on their cards. After they have danced before the group, ask them to explain which four ideas their group had and how they used them together.

ANY SIZE

The
Story

♪ **Music:** classical ballet music that tells a story

Dance games 51 and 54 had no particular stories, and these games probably produced crazy dances by skaters dancing on the spot or terrified jumpers crisscrossing the room. Sometimes these dances can create a story of their own, which you can use for a whole new dance game.

Sit the group down and together think of a theme or an idea on which you could base a story. Divide the story into a beginning, a development, and a conclusion. Think of movements that could clarify the story.

For example, if the theme is "The Fairground," the group might think of merry-go-rounds, swings, and bumper cars. Have players demonstrate movements that go with these rides.

Have the players create a dance in which they portray the story using their movement words. Remind players that a well-crafted story deals with timing, the use of space, and building tension. When the story is ready, find a piece of music, and have the players rehearse it.

Variation: Use the structure of games 51 and 54 to see what might happen before and after. For example, the terrified jumpers have some reason for being terrified. This could be the theme for an introduction dance. How will the story of the terrified jumpers end? They cannot keep on jumping forever. Find a movement solution for them.

Sound and
Dance Games

Sound and dance have been inseparable since ancient times, when sound complemented dance. Sound can support, inspire, and guide dance. It can function as a background or as something integral to building and setting a mood. The combination of sound and movement is powerful; the two together express a range of emotions to the participant as well as the observer. These games demonstrate the delightful partnership of dance and sound.

56

Dance Sentences

Materials: Pieces of paper with movement words written on them

♪ **Music:** quiet piano music

Before the session, write movement words (such as roll, leap, skip, or hop) on slips of paper.

Ask players to form a circle and pass around one of the slips of paper for everyone to read. The last person in the circle performs the action. She then adds a description or quality to the word and whispers these words to her neighbor. For example, for "roll," she may add "roll quickly," "roll and call out," or "roll with a partner." In the last case, the player next to her may choose a partner. Each person in the circle takes a turn adding another attribute to "roll." The end result should be a dance "sentence."

Form groups of four. Ask each group to create a dance sentence to music. Have the groups practice their dance and demonstrate it to the others. Which group can make the longest sentence?

57

Dancing Sound Collages

Materials: glue; scissors; old comic books, magazines, and newspapers; large pieces of cardboard

Have the players look through the periodicals and cut out exclamations, such as "crash!" "whoops!" "wow!" "wham!", that suggest a sound and cause an action. Have the group make several collages by pasting the words onto the cardboard.

Have the players choose a spot in the room to stand. Call out a word from a collage and ask the players to make a suitable movement. Call out two words, one right after the other and have the players perform two movements. Next, call out a series of ten words and ask the players to perform the movements while moving around the room. Each word should have its own movement. First, have the players dance these words in silence; then have them do the entire dance again, this time with sounds.

Finally, form groups of four and have the players create a dance from one of the collage boards. Don't forget the sounds!

The
City Awakes

Materials: A story in which many different sounds are mentioned; if necessary, write your own story

Translate the story, preferably sentence by sentence, into sound and movement sentences so that players can dance it. Here are some ideas to get you started:

- It is absolutely quiet in the street (everyone lies down silently).

- The clock strikes eight (someone imitates a clock).

- A door opens (the players open a noisy door).

- A limping child sets off for school (someone limps along and sings).

- A police siren sounds (imitate the sound and run away).

With a group of young children, you will usually have to make up a story. Older children will be able to help you make up an exciting story about what happened in the street at eight o'clock. Have the players dance a story that lasts one or two minutes. Encourage them to use their voices to make the right sounds as well.

Variation: Groups of four can rehearse the story for a few minutes and then perform it for the others.

The
Robot

Ask each player to find a space in the room. Call out the names of the parts of the body that have joints or that can make angular movements, beginning from the head and working downwards. Tell the players to stay in one spot and move the part that you mention. For example, say, "Turn your head slowly to the left, then to the right while you bend forward. Use angular movements in slow motion." Name several body parts, remembering to add "slowly and angularly."

Next, start again, from the head down. When you mention the legs, ask the players to move around the room. Tell the players they are robots and move in a particular direction, making slow and angular movements. Ask players to think of a sound to accompany each movement.

Form pairs, with one partner acting as the robot operator and the other as the robot. What story (with sounds) will each operator make the robot dance?

Fireworks

Have players stand in a circle and tell the group that they are all fireworks. Set off someone as an exploding firework by pointing to her and saying a "firework" word, such as "Pop," "Bang," or "Fizz." The chosen player jumps about in all directions. Indicate whether the player should move high in the air or low near the ground and the difference between exploding in one place and jumping around the room. Now the first player can pick another group member to be an exploding firework.

Finally, form pairs and have the partners practice a fireworks display that lasts for half a minute. Ask them to show it to the rest of the group.

Sounds Strange

Form a circle and call out strange sounds that the participants imitate. At first, loosen up the voices by making careful, quiet sounds and gradually adding more volume. Use both vowels and consonants. Ask each player to make a sound that lasts several seconds and that the others repeat.

Now everyone in the circle makes a strange sound together with a suitable movement. Then each player in turn makes a longer series of sounds and moves his way around the circle. The others imitate him. Suggest sounds that are unlike anything heard in everyday life. Children will use their imaginations and have fun with this dance game.

The
Wind

Ask everyone to find a space in the room and give the following movement instructions: "Standing in one spot, let your arm float away, just for a moment in a particular direction. Imagine a breeze that lifts your arm for an instant. Do the same thing with your head . . . shoulder . . . elbow . . . leg . . . back."

Have the players drift around the room while you make the sound of wind blowing. When the wind sound stops, tell the players to gently come to a standstill. The wind can blow the players high in the air, drifting, and also down low along the ground.

Now ask the players to make wind sounds as they dance. Tell them to imagine that they are as light as a leaf, swept up into the air to fly, drift, and fall to the ground. Let everyone see what happens to each leaf.

Tell the players that the wind is blowing harder. There is a storm. Encourage players to vocalize as they dance, and use their hands and feet to make wind sounds. Apart from the blowing sound, they can also yell out "crack!" or "ssstooooorm!"

Now tell the players there is a hurricane. The wind turns, forces the players upward, to the side, in every direction, then suddenly it pushes them down; the tempo becomes more turbulent along with the sounds. Allow the storm to blow across the room for a few minutes.

63

Dancing Sounds

Materials: objects that produce sounds (such as saucepan lids, wooden sticks, rattles, bells, and keys). Make sure that both high and low tones are represented.

Turn one side of the room into a low-tone area, and place all the objects that make a low tone in this area. Turn the other side of the room into a high-tone area, and place all the objects that make a high tone there. Put half the group in one area and the other half in the other area.

To start, a player chooses an object from her area and makes a sound (low or high, short or long), and a player in the opposite area dances to it in place. Each sound suggests a different kind of movement. Let each player have a chance to make a sound and dance to a sound.

Now one of the players in the low-tone area dances over to the other side, allowing herself to be "pushed" to the center by a sound made from a person in the low-tone area. At the center, the dancer freezes and makes a sound with her voice before she continues to dance to the other side, now guided by a sound made from a person in the high-tone area.

Have other players in turn dance in their own way to the opposite side, guided first by an object producing one type of tone, then by one making the other type of tone. Have several dancers cross over at the same time, guided by a number of noisemakers.

The
Forest
of Sound

Materials: objects that produce sounds; two footprints cut out of construction paper or cardboard

Divide the room into five zones. Area 1 is in the center and contains the two footsteps. Area 2 is a corner where a tribe of shy forest-dwellers lives. They speak only in whispers, are peaceful, make friendly sounds, and dance with care. Area 3 is a corner where a disagreeable tribe lives. They make short, hard sounds and dance with awkward movements. They cannot control their arms and legs. Area 4 is a tiny place with only a couple of inhabitants. They can no longer speak, but use a sign language. They have a couple of instruments that speak for them. Area 5 is the place where the tribe of garglers lives. They can gargle and make guttural sounds, but they can't really talk. They move like slime along the ground.

Explain the areas and their inhabitants to the players. Ask one player at a time to pick up an instrument, if they wish, and, starting from the footsteps in the middle of the room, dance through all the areas and choose a place to live, making sounds with their feet and the instrument.

When everyone has a place to live, ask each group to make a folk dance with appropriate sounds. What kinds of steps do the different tribes make? After each tribe has had time to practice, have them show the others what their dance looks and sounds like.

65

The **Dance**
of the
Instruments

Materials: a number of instruments that make sounds of varying character and volume

This game assumes that the participants have already played with instruments and know the sounds they make: A block of wood makes a short sound, a string of bells makes a tinkling sound, and so on.

Form pairs and have the partners choose one person to hold an instrument and one to move. Together, they explore the sounds of an instrument and the movements that belong with it. After a few minutes, each pair shows the group their sound and dance discoveries.

Now have the instrumentalists sit at the side of the room and the dancers stand in the center. Ask the musicians to use their instruments to dance the movers around the room. See if the movers can understand what their instrumentalist wants them to do. Does the dancer understand that he should dance down low, up high, to the side, faster, slower, more strongly, come to a stop? Have everyone change places after a few minutes.

Make groups of four and ask the group to create a conversation between the two dancers and the two musicians. What kind of a meeting will this be? What does each pair have to say to the other in sounds and movement? Have the groups demonstrate each dance and music game to the rest of the group.

66

Dance Cards II

Materials: dance cards made from paper, about three inches square

Create the dance cards before the session, or, if you like, have group members create the cards during the session. Each dance card should have a different illustration drawn or pasted on it (see the examples on page 95).

Form a circle and pass around the cards. According to the season, suggest a suitable theme (such as rain, sun, autumn, snow, storm, or early spring). Have each player show you her card and tell her the movement she should make based on the chosen theme. The player immediately does this movement. If necessary, demonstrate a dance to go with a particular card.

After everyone has practiced a movement, watch from the side of the room and encourage the players to vary the speed, force, and use of space as they repeat their movements.

Make groups of four and have each group create a dance using two or more of the members' cards. Allow them time to practice their dance before performing for the others.

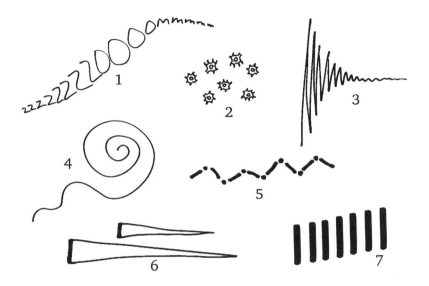

Key to illustrations:

1. a movement that gradually becomes larger or smaller

2. a short, rapid movement, performed in one spot

3. a strong movement toward silence

4. a turning movement

5. a rhythmic movement

6. an echoing movement that becomes smaller

7. heavy, short, similar movements

Puzzles with
Your Muscles

In this series of dance games, players watch, hear, and see in advance what will happen in the dance. Learning to look and see what is happening is a journey of discovery for the senses, which will be further developed through these games.

67

Three-Legged Dancing

Materials: tape, string, or ribbon

♪ **Music:** ballroom dancing music

First, practice some ballroom dancing. Players don't have to know real dance steps for this; the idea is to get the dancers moving perfectly in time to the music, using gracious movements and turns while managing to keep their heads held high and eyes up.

Then, have players choose partners and tie the right leg of one partner to the left leg of the other. When the music starts, ask the players to dance as well as before, as if nothing unusual has happened.

Variation: Change the music to circus tunes. A jury can award points to the couple who manage to remain the most poised and dignified.

68

Bottle Dance

Materials: Several plastic bottles with tops, filled with marbles or water

♪ **Music:** ballroom dancing music

Make a path through the room, marking it on each side with the plastic bottles. Have the players choose partners and stand on one side of the room.

Have pairs improvise a Viennese waltz, or something that looks like it. Ask them to dance along the pathway without knocking over any of the bottles. Extra gestures, exaggerated and with great flair, are all part of the game. After all the partners dance through once, make the path narrower and more twisting. Who knocks over the fewest number of bottles? Dim the lights: can the dancers still hear and see what they are doing?

Orange Dance

Materials: oranges

♪ **Music:** any kind of dance music

Place oranges between the foreheads of two players, then start the dance music. Ask the partners to dance and keep the orange between their foreheads for at least twenty seconds.

Variations: Try apples, eggs, and bananas. You can also use tennis balls or balloons.

Broom Dance

Materials: a broom

♪ **Music:** pop music (Top 40 hits) or ballroom dancing music; a fast piece and a slow piece

Not everyone finds it easy to dance, particularly at the beginning of a party or a school dance. Take the broom and dance around the room with it. Pass the broom to another player and take a partner for yourself. Encourage the person with the broom to dance with it, then give it to someone else after choosing a human partner. Within a very short time, the whole group will be dancing and the broom can be set aside.

71

Confetti
and Balloons

Materials: balloons, confetti

♪ **Music:** one slow and one fast tune

Give everyone a balloon and play some fast music. Encourage players to dance around the room while keeping their balloon in the air. Each player should make the balloon an integral part of his dance improvisation. The balloons should not touch the floor.

Have the players choose partners, volleying the balloon from one to the other as part of the dance. Finally, play a slow piece of music and have partners hold a balloon between them, on their chests, backs, or foreheads. Can they move the balloon up and down and along their bodies while dancing?

Variation: For a festive touch, fill the balloons with confetti: there will be an instant party atmosphere if they burst!

The Hat Dance

Materials: a hat; makeup or ribbons

♪ **Music:** swing music, or pop music with a swinging beat

Have everyone find a place in the room and ask one person to start and stop the music. Put on the hat and, when the music starts, dance around the room for about a minute. With a grand gesture, place the hat on someone else's head. Have players dance and pass the hat from one head to the next. When the music stops, everyone stands still. Whoever is wearing the hat is out and is given a stripe of makeup on her cheek or a ribbon to wear.

Start again. Put on the hat and find someone else to wear it. Make sure that no one starts running; otherwise the passing of the hat doesn't count.

Try the dance with slow-motion music and see how the players' bodies move differently.

73

The
Clothes Dance

Materials: clothing and accessories from the players; a large basket; blanket

♪ **Music:** swinging music

Place the basket in the middle of the room and ask players to put on their coats, hats, and other outer wear.

After the players have warmed up, play the music and have everyone dance around the room. As they pass the basket, tell them to remove their coat, tie, scarf, glove, or other outer garment and deposit it into the basket while dancing.

When the basket is full, hold the blanket over the top of the basket. Have players dance by the basket again, reach under the blanket, and take out a garment. Remind players to keep

dancing using continuous movements while picking out a garment. The owner of that garment becomes the partner of the player who picked it, and they dance together for a while. The two dancers can either decide to stay together as partners or take a new piece of clothing from the basket and dance with their new partner.

This dance is also good as an introduction game.

74

Whose Is It?

♪ **Music:** pop or disco music

Materials: a screen or sheet large enough to hide half of the group

Set up the screen at one side of the dance floor. Ask half of the group to hide behind the screen. Have the players behind the screen stick a hand, nose, or earlobe over or around the screen one at a time. Tell members of the other group to dance by the screen, hold onto the extended body part and dance with the other player. Then have them guess who they are dancing with. If they are right, the other player must come out from behind the screen.

The
Dance Quiz

Materials: cans of soft drinks or fruit juices

♪ **Music:** Top 40 tunes

This game can be used as an interval between other dances during a dance session based on pop music. Play it with children and young adults who can sing some Top 40 hits and with parents who are familiar with the music.

Play an extract from a song. The first person to correctly guess the title gets a drink and is the first on the dance floor. Ask the others to join in after the first few steps. Repeat with another song.

This game works well when the participants are used to it. After the first time, players will know the rules and be prepared.

Variation: For a more challenging game, have the participants sing along when you stop the music or turn down the volume. Whoever sings along best (with or without a microphone) while dancing wins a drink.

Musical Chairs with Obstacles

Materials: old chairs; boxes; tape, string, or ribbon

♪ **Music:** any fun dance music

Set up the chairs in a row along one wall. Use one less chair than the number of players. Have players choose a partner and dance around the room when the music begins. (If you have an odd-numbered group, have one players form a group of three with two other players.) When the music stops, have players run quickly to a chair and sit down. The person who is left out sits out. Remove one of the chairs and start the music again.

Variations:

- Have players dance toward the chairs when the music stops instead of running.

- For a sillier variation, tie the right leg of one partner to the left leg of the other. If both partners don't find a chair, both players are out of the game.

- Use sturdy boxes in place of chairs. See how quickly and carefully the players can sit down without breaking the boxes.

Story Dances

━━━◢

Dance games are often developed from a story, although not every story can be easily interpreted as a dance. Telling a story in movement means that the dancers must translate the actions in the plot into movement words.

Dancers add the elements of dance—time (tempo), power, and space—to create a living dance story. In particular, each dance story must contain a clear beginning, development, and conclusion. The dance stories described here are suitable for toddlers and young children, and provide ideas on how you can develop an existing story into a dance. Throughout each dance story, talk to the players and help them visualize the story through dance movements.

The
Great Forest
of Trees

♪ **Music:** slow ballet, new age music, or jazz

Play dance game 20, "Drifting Leaves, Growing Trees" as an introduction to this game. Then have players sing a song about trees. (If no suitable song exists, write words and adapt them to a well-known tune.) As players sing, have them slowly dance together and disperse again. Tell them that they are tree branches growing thicker and thinner. Have them make flowing movements and hold each other by the wrists as they all come together.

The dance story begins when all the players are close, holding onto one another's wrists. Suddenly, the branches of the tree grow away from each other. Some branches stop growing, others grow upward, downward, or along the ground. Touch some players, who will then freeze; give others a growing potion, so they grow thicker. Have other players gradually grow into a knot or push over and under the other branches. Some can get stuck against the others. On your signal, everyone jumps apart and moves along the ground like tree roots. As roots, the players no longer have power in their arms.

The
Great Forest
of People

Materials: pictures of trees

♪ **Music:** slow, rhythmic music

Ask the players to dance while imagining they are a large, broad tree. Some players should dance the branches, others dance the roots, and still others dance the leaves. The branches, roots, and leaves become tangled and the dancers come to a standstill. Unravel the branches, roots, and leaves and toss them, one by one, out into the room. Throw some in one direction, into a pile. Throw others in other directions, so that a handful of piles are formed.

Start the music and explain that the roots and branches landed in magic places. Each pile is the beginning of a new tree, and each tree is different. Ask each group to invent a tree, such as a willow, an oak, or a pine. (You may want to show the group pictures of trees to help them visualize different kinds.)

During the dance, encourage the players to give their human tree enough space, power, and time in which to grow in the roots, leaves, and branches. Ask each group to demonstrate their tree to the rest of the players. Some of the players could be elves and dance through forest.

The
Shopping Street

Materials: a shopping bag for each player; a recording of sounds on a street with many shops, preferably a market, with people shopping, children shouting, and so on

♪ **Music:** a piece ranging from slow to fast tempos

Ask each player to find a place in the room and tell them that they are all part of a busy street scene. At your signal, ask players to dash across the room from one place to another. When they pass by another person, they move into a higher gear and go faster.

Now, ask players to crisscross through the room, alternating high and low movements. But this time, when a player passes someone else, they feel as if they have syrup on their shoes; it is hard to go on.

Give each player a shopping bag and have them dance through the shopping street, buying all kinds of things in the stores. They dance through the streets—fast, faster, hurry, hurry—because everyone wants to buy everything in town. The players go into a shop and out again; each time, their bags get heavier. Have them dance more and more slowly until they are dragging themselves and their bags along the ground or even crawling.

Repeat the busy street scene, but now have players do their shopping in pairs with one bag. Sometimes they both see something they want at the same time. They dance high and low, bending forward or stretching up for things they can't quite reach, and suddenly they see a friend they want to wave to.

Play the tape of the shopping street and ask each pair to make a shopping dance, showing who they meet in town, how they greet each other, and how they fill the shopping bag.

Little Red Riding Hood and the Wolf

Materials: a copy of the story with illustrations

♪ **Music:** slow film or classical music

Read the story to the group, then warm up the players with the following instructions: *First, let's warm up our feet so that we can go into the forest. Go eight paces on your heels, eight paces on the outside of your feet, eight paces on the insteps, hop forward, backward, and sideways. Pause, and then begin again, sometimes lightly, then more heavily.*

For the duration of the musical extract, have all the players move like Red Riding Hood, skipping without fear through the steadily darkening forest. She dances along every little path, first long, straight paths, then short twisting paths. Little Red Riding Hood hops lightly, carefully, and happily. She is curious.

Play another musical fragment to help players dance the Wolf's sly, crafty steps. The Wolf creeps low along the ground, slowly, sometimes darting quickly forward, or hiding behind imaginary bushes. His footsteps are fast, large, expansive, and touch down softly.

Now play a piece of music that combines the two characteristics, and dance the meeting of Red Riding Hood and the Wolf, first as a group, then with just two players. The group can decide and rehearse how the story should end. Is there one wolf or ten? Perhaps there are three Super Red Riding Hoods who overcome the Wolf.

The
Little Man
in
Trashcanland

Materials: a toy drum; a doll; paper chains or crepe-paper streamers for each player

♪ **Music:** music that begins softly, builds up to percussion

Tell the story and encourage players to act out the character's actions. For young children, use the drum and doll to help them visualize the story. *Once upon a time there was a man in Trashcanland who lived in a big green drum. Every morning the drum opened up and the man crept out.* The players stretch out, make themselves very large, very small, huddle up, make themselves fat, then thin. *He rolled himself up like a worm and stretched himself out several times, each time differently.* Players roll themselves up and then stretch out.

In Trashcanland there was a big heap of trash. The players jump over, to the left, forward, backward, to the side of an imaginary pile of trash. *The man wanted to clean up the mess.* The players help him. *The man was so happy that he decided to have a party and dance with a streamer.* Give each player a paper chain or streamer and ask them to imitate the man. Play the music and encourage them to throw their streamer up, bring it downward in a curve, around the body, and so on. Finally, in small groups, ask the players to make up a streamer dance to music.

The
World
of Goblins

Materials: a book about goblins

♪ **Music:** rhythmic, electronic pop music

Read the book about goblins to the group. Suggest that the players act out the following scenes: *Goblins get up early in the morning and are very friendly toward each other. They stand in long rows opposite each other and rub bottoms, noses, hands, feet, and backs against each other. After breakfast, they clean their houses. But today someone has hidden the broom and the duster. The goblins decide to clean with their hands and feet. They make large rubbing movements across the floor and walls with their*

arms and skate with their feet. They roll on their backs or stomachs on the floor, first in one place, then all over. Now the room is so clean that the goblins can slip and slide around, forward, backward, and sideways.

When the goblins return to their houses, they have to clamber through the tree roots, over and under. Have half of the players form a network of roots, some lying down, some standing, and some hanging. Who can dance through the roots without touching any of them? The group of roots and the group of dancers then change places.

Next, in groups of four, have the players dance around the room; three of the group are roots and one dances through them. Finally, each group performs a dance of goblins for the others to watch.

Goblin Caps

Materials: caps decorated with paper; a tambourine

Have players act out the following movements: *The goblins often have to make themselves smaller, folding themselves up to climb, crawl, and slip through the grass. They "shrink" so they can move through a narrow passageway, beginning with one hand and then following with all parts of the body. When they are through the passageway, they stretch out, twisting in all kinds of contortions, very slowly, and move along to another spot.*

Use the tambourine to warn that the goblins' enemies are around. Have players freeze, wait, then group together.

Give a cap to each player and have them put it on. Tell them that it is a very windy day (make wind sounds with the tambourine or with your voice). The wind is constantly blowing the caps off. Have the players try to catch their caps while the wind blows them along. The wind blows them higher and higher; use beats of the tambourine to increase the tension. The wind blows from behind, blowing them forward and backward; they have to cling to each other so they're not blown away. The wind drops and evening comes. They roll on the ground in twos or threes, and fall asleep.

84

Newspaper Dance

Materials: newspapers; two-sided tape; a piece of Velcro or some kind of natural sticky seed pods or burrs that may also be used as a percussion instrument

♪ **Music:** classical symphony

Before the game, tear long strips of newspaper and put the two-sided tape on some of the strips. Keep one sheet of newspaper intact to use in the first part of the game.

To begin, take the sheet of newspaper and tell the following short story. *It is the first day of school. Keisha is very nervous. She notices that everyone has a notebook with them, except for her. She carefully takes a notebook from the teacher, but it tears when she picks it up.*

Tear up some of the newspaper and have the players turn with "tearing" movements around the room, sometimes quickly, others slowly. Ask them to listen carefully to the movement words in the story. Tell them that when you stop tearing they should stop moving and freeze on the spot.

Keisha keeps on tearing the book by accident. One piece tears straight, another crooked. Place the long strips of newspaper around the room. Start the music and have the players dance around the room avoiding the paper strips, balancing their way between the strips or jumping over them. Finally, have players roll around on the paper and get well and truly stuck.

Show the piece of Velcro or the burr to the group and explain how it sticks to things. Form pairs and have the partners hook on to each other in the same way, rolling around the room, dancing free, sticking to someone else.

Ask the players: How do you stick to someone else? Encourage them to make beautiful and strange balancing forms with their body. Have everyone watch pairs who have discovered strange ways of sticking together and dancing.

Variation: Try using whole newspapers stuck to the players' bodies. Have them tear the newspaper while they dance.

85

Tumbling
and
Tossing Wasps

Materials: pictures of wasps in various stages of development

♪ **Music:** classical or ragtime music

Begin by showing pictures of wasps to the group. Have the players look closely at the wasp's body.

As you tell the following story, have the players dance each line with the appropriate movement. With very young children, signal changes in movements and directions. *Once upon a time there was a wasp who couldn't find anywhere to hide from daylight or from her enemies. She prowled, climbed, turned herself around on the ground and in the hollow of a branch. She made everything around her hollow and round. She pulled pieces of bark over herself for warmth. With her back, feet, and head, she pushed the pieces forward and backward.*

Then, the wasp became bigger and was thrown out of the tree, burrow and all. Have the dancers fall down and to the side; one wasp after the other is tossed to the side, some high, some low. *The wasp tumbles and tosses further in different directions.*

Start the music and retell the story. Again, have the dancers follow the movement words.

Next, form pairs and have one of the partners swing and dance high in the air while the other dances and tumbles low on the ground. Tell the pair to stay together while following one another around the room. They dance high and low while stumbling and trying to use each other as supports.

Snail Dance

Materials: pictures of snails

♪ **Music:** piano music

Show the pictures of the snails to the group. Encourage players to dance the movement words as you create the following scene:

One day a sleepy snail takes a wrong turn and lands on a sand bank, which to him is like a desert. The snail wakes up and stretches himself in all directions. He moves himself forward and pulls himself along, in and out, gets fatter and thinner. He glides forward, crawls along very low on the ground. He zigzags, curls up, turns, and gets stuck in the loose sand. The snail cannot move. Which animal can help him?

Ask players to show how another animal or group of animals moves. The players should keep silent, showing the animal through movement only. Have the players decide which animal can best help the snail and finish the story. Have players dance out the entire story, first in silence, then to music.

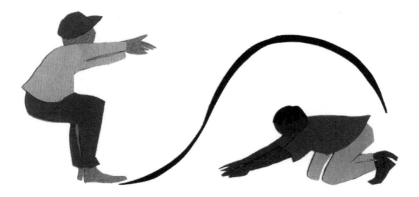

Party Dances

This group of dance games is for special occasions. Just about any celebration, however, lends itself to a dance game.

Reindeer
and
Santa Claus
Helpers

Materials: boxes or cones

♪ **Music:** lively classical music; lively Christmas music

Ask the players to sing a holiday song, such as "Jingle Bells," as they dance around like reindeer, with trotting steps, lifting their legs high. Place the boxes or cones on the floor to represent chimneys and start the music. Have other players dance between the obstacles on the roof, being Santa's helpers and trying not to fall off the roof. Encourage them to stumble over their feet and make funny clowning gestures. Santa Claus has told them to step carefully across the narrow edges of the roof.

At your signal, the dancers switch back and forth between dancing reindeer steps and helper steps. Indicate differences in direction, speed, and power.

Finally, ask each of Santa's crew to dance a solo and show all his tricks and capers.

Holiday Candles

Materials: candles; matches; pictures of stars

♪ **Music:** instrumental holiday music

Light a candle, dim the lights, and move your hand over the candle to show the group how the rays from the flame flicker across the room: straight up in the air, diagonally, flowing to one side or the other. Ask the players to dance these movements in an even tempo. Have them vary the tempo and accelerate their speed. Like the candle, the players can dance high and low, making ducking movements up and down.

But candles falter sometimes, the flame hangs still in the air for a moment before flickering. Have the players make short stops every now and then, freeze for a moment, and then continue on.

Put up the pictures of stars around the room and start the music. When the players pass one, have them shine their "flame" more strongly and brightly in their movements.

89

Doughnut Dance

Materials: information on how doughnuts are made

♪ **Music:** cartoon music of different tempos

Talk about how doughnuts are made. Have the players be doughnuts and try out different ways of rolling: forward, backward, over the shoulder with the head to one side, with a lot of power, or very floppily. Doughnuts are sometimes hard, sometimes squishy, and often have strange shapes. Each type of doughnut has a different movement form.

Next, the players prepare to be shaped and cooked. Each player is a piece of dough that is transformed from a long flat shape into a round ball, and they dance this process. Then the doughnuts go into the hot oil: they are turned slowly and change speed and size as they cook. Doughnuts bounce up when they hit the hot oil; the players throw themselves upward from the ground and land softly to show how the doughnut moves in the pan.

Then, they splash out of the pan, spattering in every direction, coming to rest for a moment, jumping from the floor, landing again, and rolling around.

Practice doughnut dancing in pairs: jumping, landing, rolling, and shooting away.

Variation: Instead of doughnuts, have players move like fireworks, popcorn, or boiling oil.

Ghosts
at the Fair

🎵 **Music:** cartoon or circus music

Ask players to remember a time they went to a fair. Have them recall the sights, sounds, and smells; the people, the rides, and the attractions. If some of the players have never been to a fair, ask others to explain the layout at a fairground (including rides, food booths, and side-show attractions).

Play the music. Have the players move along in a conga line, holding on to each other as they pass the fairground attractions, gazing at the wide variety of booths and rides. As the music plays, the dancers move with more and more excitement, getting caught up in the mood of the fair. Have them let go of each other and dance to the different things each wants to see. For instance, one player wants to stop at the merry-go-

round; he dances in a circle. The bumper cars excite another player; she bumps into invisible obstacles and moves on again in another direction.

After everyone finds an attraction to dance to, throw sheets over a few players, turning them into ghosts. The ghosts dance, haunting others in the group and making ghostly passes around the rides and booths. Ghosts can have their own dance, or they can dance how a ghost would experience the different rides and attractions at the fair.

91

Carnival

Materials: homemade or store-bought carnival masks of different animals

♪ **Music:** carnival or caribbean music

Set the masks along one side of the room and play the music. Ask the players to dance as if they were in a procession of clowns, pulling funny faces and making silly movements. They trip, just manage to catch themselves, stumble on, and so on. Have the procession slow down. As the procession of clowns dances slower and slower, the clowns change into an animal, such as a cat.

Hold up each mask and dance a few steps that go with each one; have the players mimic your movements. After you have shown several masks (clowns, cats, monsters—whatever), let the players choose their own masks and put them on. Tell them to first move in slow motion to be sure they don't bump into each other and to get used to seeing through the masks. Finally, have small groups form their own dancing procession.

Concentration Dances

"Watch what you're doing." "You're not looking." "Watch where you're going." Everyone's familiar with these exclamations telling us our attention has slipped. Concentration is something that people can develop, however, and dancing is helpful. Dancers are constantly reminded of the presence of other people and obstacles that can slow them down. Watching others, reacting to their way of dancing, listening to the sounds another person makes, hearing someone coming, and remaining concentrated on movements all sharpen concentration skills.

92

Slowly Moving Scenes

♪ **Music:** slow, rhythmic music

This game is a continuation of dance game 46, "Living Statues." Ask the players to slowly dance around the room, making statues here and there. Have them begin as recognizable statues, dance toward a position, and slowly come to a stop in a characteristic posture, such as a traffic cop with arms outstretched. Have them hold this pose, then move again and stop as another statue, perhaps a ballerina in arabesque or a fisherman casting a line. The object is to transition from one character to another, dancing to music with a slow tempo.

Form small groups and have the players make a very gradual transition in movements, from statue to statue, as if part of a movie. The statues don't have to have any connection to each other; the emphasis is on changes of form that are danced in an extremely slow tempo.

93

The
Photo Album

Materials: photos of a person at different ages, from childhood to adulthood

♪ **Music:** slow, electronic music

This game is also a continuation of game number 46, "Living Statues." Show players the photographs and ask them to make up a life story.

Begin the music and have players create poses as infants, young children, adults, and elderly people. Have them dance by moving slowly from one pose to the next, spending a second or two on each transition, so that they "grow up" through the series of portraits.

Ask the players to form small groups and have each group create a "life story" dance to perform for the others. How do they show important life events or life stages?

94

Stand-In Dance

♪ **Music:** a long piece of music that has plenty of variety (such as music by Stravinsky or Beethoven)

This dance is most successful only after the players have practiced a number of other dance games. The players should be able to work independently and dance in a variety of tempos, power, and space configurations.

Have the players count off, and play the music. Ask the first player to dance on a particular subject. The second player watches this dancer for half a minute or so and then calls out "stop" when she thinks she knows the subject of the dance. She then takes over, continuing where the first dancer left off. The third player watches and guesses the theme, and the game continues until everyone has had a chance to dance.

Variation:

- Have the second player join in with the first dancer. The two improvise as a couple. Encourage other dancers to join until half of the group is dancing and the others are spectators.

Roll Back
the
Film

Materials: a reel-to-reel or other tape recorder on which you can play music backwards

♪ **Music:** film music

Form small groups and ask the players to make up a dance that tells a short story. Tell them that the introduction should consist of between three and five images; the development, six to eight images; and the conclusion a few more. Have them join these images together to make a dance. Give the groups time to rehearse the dance to the music so that they know exactly what order the images go in.

Now, play the music backwards and have the groups perform their dance backwards, from the final image to the start of the story. Have them perform it for the rest of the group. If performing the whole dance backwards is too difficult, have the groups split up the dance and perform it in shorter parts.

Lighten Up and Illuminate

Materials: a few spotlights

♪ **Music:** complex synthesizer or symphonic rock music

Darken the room as much as possible and direct a few spotlights toward the floor, creating pools of light. Have players dance from one pool of light to the next. When in the light, they dance as busily as they can; in the darker areas, they dance slowly. When the dancers are accustomed to dancing in the darkened areas, have them dance slowly in the light pools as well, as though an image is moving in slow motion. Then, tell them to move like a flash into the light and make a sudden stop, so that there are big contrasts in tempo.

Next, have the players dance a circuit around the space, showing them where to change tempo, where to change height, where to dance in the spotlight, and where to swing through the room. If they run into someone in a spotlight, they should instantly dance off in the opposite direction. If they meet in the shadow, have them dance together in "shadow meetings," becoming each other's shadow.

Form small groups and ask each group to create dances in which the players move from the dark into the light. Have someone dance into the light; the others are his shadow and can reproduce his movements in the dark, but a little more vaguely. The contrast between clear and vague is striking to see.

Cat Dance

Materials: pictures of a cat

♪ **Music:** orchestra music or film music

To begin, show the group the cat pictures. Then, ask the players to lie down on the floor like sleeping cats. (Make sure the floor is clean and warm.) Talk to the players and encourage them to move as cat-like as possible: *Slowly the cats awaken and stretch themselves. They see something but are still too sleepy to pay it much attention. They don't make a sound.*

Suggest that players think about how cats move: *They scratch their noses with a paw, lick their legs, and stretch out a foot. They stand, arch their back, and sink back to the ground. They stand up again and walk, which is like dancing on cushions. They move to another spot and stretch out one back leg, then the other.*

Form small groups and have each group dance like cats. Tell them to discuss which cat movements to use; four per player is probably enough. Encourage them to use the entire room and show variations in speed.

98

Flashlight Dance

Materials: flashlights

♪ **Music:** various kinds of film music; staccato music

Have the players whirl like lightning from one spot in the room to another, changing from high to low as they whirl, turn, zigzag, and whiz from place to place. Ask dancers to find three or four movements they feel comfortable with. They dance them from the ground or from a high position and show the suddenness with which they begin and end.

Divide the players into pairs and dim the lights. Have one partner be a shaft of light, the other, the shadow. The shadow follows the light exactly. Have partners change places after a minute or two.

Give a flashlight to each pair and darken the room. Ask the light to dance along in front while the shadow imitates her and shines the flashlight on her. Make sure that the first dancer is illuminated with enough light. After changing roles, have the shadows illuminate their partner from one side of the room. The lights dance around the room, flashing from one place to the next, using a few movements that they dance at various levels. They should work with the shadows cast on the walls, moving toward the wall from the dark side of the room. Have the partners switch roles again.

Next, have the shadows shine their flashlight on a single dancer in her journey into and away from the light. Watch a few soloists at a time. Then combine "flashes of light" and "shadows": have two dancers work together in the light and the shade; the flashlights fall on them, and another pair immediately follows them.

Binoculars

Materials: homemade binoculars made of toiletpaper rolls with colored cellophane attached to the ends; a telescope made of rolled-up paper or cardboard; or real binoculars

♪ **Music:** pop music

Play the music and ask players to improvise three movements: collapsing, stretching out, and draining away. Using tempo, power, and space, have them demonstrate their improvisations to the other players. Their movements may not yet be a set pattern; they may only be an idea that the dancers can develop further.

Now form pairs. One partner is the dancer, the other holds binoculars and is the observer. Tell the observers to use the binoculars to look at details; for instance, pay special attention to the hands. The observer watches and gives constructive suggestions or asks questions of the dancer after he has fin-

ished: How did he use his hands? How did he use his torso? Perhaps his legs could demonstrate more power when he is collapsing.

Now the players change roles: the observer becomes the dancer and other partner gives feedback. Have the pairs demonstrate their dances to the rest of the group. Has each dance improved after doing a concentration exercise with the help of an observer?

Choreography
for a
Blind Dancer

Materials: a blindfold

♪ **Music:** slow, rhythmic electronic music

The idea of this game is that a dance that was created as part of another game is used as a starting point for a deeper study of the dance.

Divide the group into pairs; have one partner be the teacher and the other, the student. Ask teachers to think of a dance to teach their student. The students, however, must act as if they cannot hear, see, or speak. If each student agrees, have them wear a blindfold. The teachers must convey their dance nonverbally and with a great deal of feeling. They will have to "demonstrate" every step and movement and let their partner feel precisely what each movement is and what the next step will be.

When the students have learned their dance, the pair perform the dance together. The student stands in front of the teacher, with her eyes open if she wishes, and dances into the room first, followed by the teacher, who sees only then if her teaching is successful.

101

Different Dance Locations

Materials: a sound-system for each dance location; spot-lights and flashlights; various props such as boxes, streamers, fans, sheets

♪ **Music:** various pieces, one for each dance location

Some dances can be prepared in such a way that they can be performed in places other than a room or a stage. Before the game, set up several dance locations. Set up music on a landing or by a spiral staircase. In a darkened hallway, set up music and spotlights. Provide flashlights. Use props and music and choose sites in various spots around the building if possible.

Divide the players into small groups and ask each group to find a dance location and create a dance that the space and music inspire. The dancers may have the same theme, but the performances will be different. The players on the staircase could hear other players come in below and dance away. In the darkened hallway, dancers might use spotlights or flashlights to see one another or they may simply listen to their steps.

Encourage the groups to create dances that will surprise spectators because of the out-of-ordinary space they have chosen. Watching, hearing, seeing, and feeling become an extra activity during the enjoyment of the performance.

The dances need not last longer than a minute. Have the rest of the group move from one dance location to the next, observing each other's dances.

Appendix: Creating Your Own Dances

While the 101 dance games in this book will provide you with hours of inspiring, rewarding play, use the following guidelines to create your own dance games. First are some thoughts on how dance can take on a variety of shapes and forms, followed by an example of how to create a particular type of children's dance game.

Dancing involves the following aspects:

- **Tempo:** Dancing can be quick, slow, accelerated, and include moments when you stop. You can dance to a particular count, time, or rhythm. The pace can vary enormously.

- **Power:** You can dance in a very relaxed way or with much tension. You can, for instance, act very strong or be quite limp. In a dance game, energy—or the lack of it—can equally influence how a dance looks.

- **Space:** You can dance in one spot or all across the room. In dance you work with directions and levels (for example, you do not always dance at the same height) and you can dance with the space you make with your body.

- **Energy:** Your body is the instrument that dances. The dance is dependent on how your body feels and how much energy you can summon for the activity.

- **Movement words:** You make all sorts of movements with your body: your body works, performs, acts, and "speaks" with movement words. You can be shy, arrogant, brutal, courteous, or cheerful in the way your body moves.

- **Variation:** You can dance with or without music, with drumrolls, drumbeats, instruments, or music on tapes or CDs. You can dance in daytime, under artificial light, with spotlights, or with the use of a camera. You can dance through a story, ideas, feelings, and thoughts. You can dance with tables, chairs, sticks, and pieces of cloth.

Step-by-step Dance Games

Say you want to create a dance about a children's story entitled "The Caterpillar."

First, make a list of the kinds of movements a caterpillar makes, including rolling over, moving forward, turning, curling up, and stretching out. These are movement words. You can roll quickly or slowly (tempo); you can roll with a relaxed movement, but still do it quickly (tempo and power). You can roll quickly, in a relaxed way but without moving around very much (space). Continue developing ideas from the story. Movement words are especially suggestive. Embellish these words with the elements of dance mentioned above.

Here's another example:

The story of Alice in Wonderland concerns a young girl who travels through a magical land, meeting all sorts of characters. All the characters in the story can be translated into movements, including Alice, the White Rabbit, the Queen of Hearts, the Cheshire Cat, and the Mad Hatter. How does Alice move?

She skips down a path: movement word

She skips, sometimes quickly, then more slowly: tempo

She skips quickly and easily: power

She skips from one place to the other: space

Sometimes she pauses for a moment, then skips to the left, then skips to the right, and then straight ahead again: space

She skips very gracefully and fluidly: movement words

She skips and sings a song or hears a melody: music variation

She skips and picks up a flower to wave from side to side; she throws it into the air as she dances: movement variation

Thus Alice's part in the dance game grows. Each figure in the story can be similarly "moved" or danced, and each participant can dance each role. Create extra roles for a larger group. In the Alice in Wonderland story, for example, the trees could also move.

Index

101 MUSIC GAMES FOR CHILDREN *by* Jerry Storms

For playing with children ages 4 and up

Music is wonderful for bringing out creativity and encouraging learning in kids. They love to sing and dance, and they love it when adults sing and dance along with them. Appropriate for families, teachers, day care providers, and camp leaders, this book presents lively music games that children and adults can play together.

Using popular songs, easy rhythms, and musical recordings, the games in this book help children develop creative, personal, and social skills. They also learn about music and sound. The games are not competitive — they encourage and reward children for participating, not for winning.

Part of the **SmartFun Books** series that brought you 101 DANCE GAMES FOR CHILDREN, the games in 101 MUSIC GAMES FOR CHILDREN help to develop:

- Listening and trust
- Concentration and improvisation
- Group interaction and expression

NO SPECIAL MUSICAL KNOWLEDGE OR INSTRUMENTS NEEDED

All you need to play the 101 music games are music tapes or CDs and simple instruments, many of which kids can have fun making from common household items. Age levels are suggested for each game ranging from four years old to teens and up. Many games are especially good for large group settings such as birthday parties and day care. Others are easily adapted to meet classroom needs.

This book also makes a great gift. Grandparents, parents, teachers — anyone who enjoys interacting with children — will love it.

More than 160,000 copies sold in 11 languages worldwide

Author **Jerry Storms** was a professional music teacher for thirteen years and a professor at the Royal Conservatory in The Hague. He has written several popular books on playing and performing music with children. His books have been published in 11 languages around the world. He currently lives in the Netherlands.

160 pages ... 30 illus. ... Paperback $11.95 ... Spiral bound $14.95

To order please see last page or call (800) 266-5592

GROWTH AND RECOVERY WORKBOOKS FOR CHILDREN *by* Wendy Deaton, MFCC, and Ken Johnson, Ph.D.

A creative, child-friendly program **for children ages 6–12,** these popular workbooks are filled with original exercises to foster healing, self-understanding, and optimal growth. They are written by a winning author team for professionals to use in their work with children.

The Workbook is designed for one-on-one use between child and professional. Tasks are balanced between writing and drawing, left and right brain, thinking and feeling, and are keyed to the phases and goals of therapy: creating a therapeutic alliance—exploring delayed reactions—teaching coping strategies—integrating and strength-building.

Each Workbook is formatted to become the child's very own, with plenty of space to write and draw, friendly line drawings, and a place for the child's name right on the colorful cover. Each also comes with a "Therapist's Guide" which includes helpful references to Dr. Johnson's book *Trauma in the Lives of Children* (see previous page).

Each Workbook is available as a **Practitioner Pack** for easy page-by-by reproductions (call for more details).

Titles in the series include:

NO MORE HURT provides children who have been physically or sexually abused a "safe place" to explore their feelings.

LIVING WITH MY FAMILY helps children traumatized by domestic violence and family quarrels identify and express their fears.

SOMEONE I LOVE DIED is for children who have lost a loved one and are dealing with grieving and loss.

A SEPARATION IN MY FAMILY is for children whose parents are separating or have already separated or divorced.

DRINKING AND DRUGS IN MY FAMILY is for children with family members who engage in regular alcohol and substance abuse.

MY OWN THOUGHTS AND FEELINGS SERIES: Three exploratory workbooks for use with younger children (ages 6–10): FOR YOUNG GIRLS and FOR YOUNG BOYS are for problems of depression, low self-esteem, and maladjustment; ON STOPPING THE HURT is for young children who may have suffered physical or emotional abuse.

A selection of Behavioral Science Book Service

Workbooks $8.95 each ... Practitioner Packs $17.95 each

***For special discounts and additional information
please call Hunter House at (800) 266-5592***

ORDER FORM

10% DISCOUNT on orders of $50 or more —
20% DISCOUNT on orders of $150 or more —
30% DISCOUNT on orders of $500 or more —
On cost of books for fully prepaid orders

NAME

ADDRESS

CITY/STATE   ZIP/POSTAL CODE

PHONE   COUNTRY (outside U.S.A.)

TITLE	QTY		PRICE	TOTAL
101 Dance Games for Children (paperback)	I	@	$11.95	
101 Dance Games for Children (spiral bound)	I	@	$14.95	
101 Music Games for Children (paperback)	I	@	$11.95	
101 Music Games for Children (spiral bound)	I	@	$14.95	
Please list other titles below:				
	I	@	$	
	I	@	$	
	I	@	$	
	I	@	$	
	I	@	$	
	I	@	$	
	I	@	$	

Shipping costs:
First book: $2.50 ($6.00 outside U.S.)
Each additional book: $.75 ($3.00 outside U.S.)
For UPS rates and bulk orders call us at (510) 865-5282

TOTAL	
Less discount @_____%	(_____)
TOTAL COST OF BOOKS	
Calif. residents add sales tax	
Shipping & handling	
TOTAL ENCLOSED	
Please pay in U.S. funds only	

❑ Check   ❑ Money Order   ❑ Visa   ❑ M/C   ❑ Discover

Card # _____ Exp date _____

Signature _____

Complete and mail to:
Hunter House Inc., Publishers
PO Box 2914, Alameda CA 94501-0914
Orders: 1-800-266-5592
Phone (510) 865-5282 Fax (510) 865-4295

❑ Check here to receive our book catalog

HDG 1/96